DAY HIKING SEQUOIA

Fifty Day Hikes for Sequoia National Park

by

Steve Sorensen

Second Edition, completely revised

Fuyu Press
PO Box 720
Three Rivers, CA 93271

Day Hiking Sequoia

Fifty Day Hikes for Sequoia National Park

by

Steve Sorensen

Second Edition, completely revised

Published by **Fuyu Press**
     PO Box 720
     Three Rivers, CA 93271

WARNING AND DISCLAIMER

Every effort has been made to provide the most accurate maps and information for this guidebook. However, as with any outdoor sport, hiking has a potential for injury. The author and publisher of this guidebook accept no responsibility for bodily injury or loss of property by hikers using this guidebook. Hikers must exercise caution and common sense at all times.

Table of Contents

INTRODUCTION

THE FOOTHILLS

GIANT FOREST

LODGEPOLE

DORST CREEK

MINERAL KING

APPENDICES

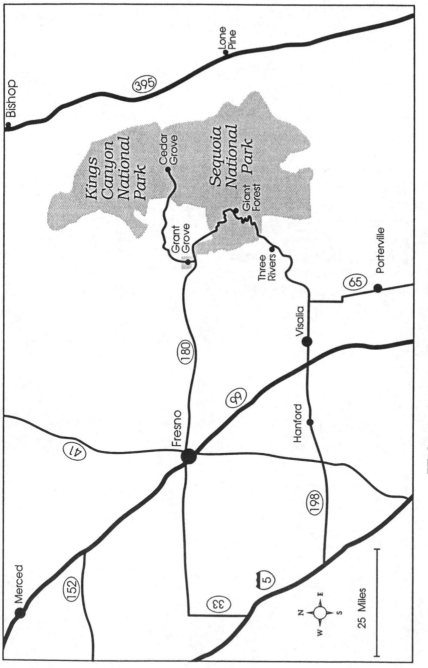

Highway Access to Sequoia National Park

Map Legend

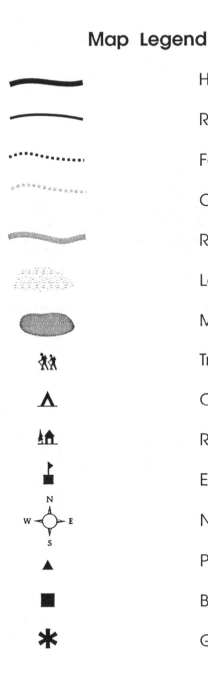

Highway

Road

Featured Trail

Other Trail

River or Creek

Lake

Meadow

Trailhead

Campground

Ranger Station

Entrance Station

North Symbol

Peak

Building

Giant Sequoia

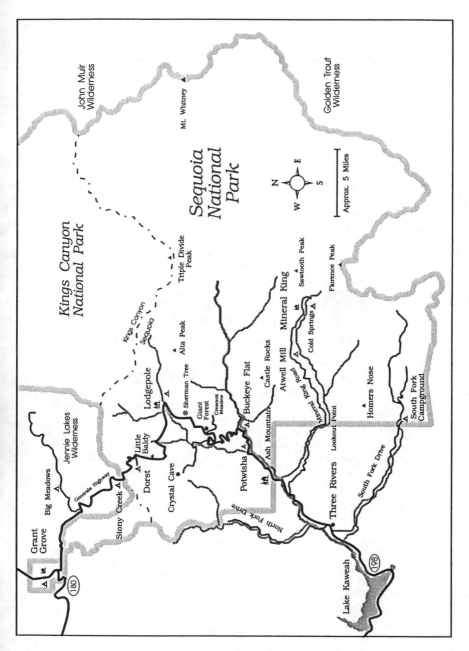

Sequoia National Park

INTRODUCING

SEQUOIA NATIONAL PARK

All too often, the first thing visitors to Sequoia National Park ask is, "Where's the tree you drive through?" The second question they ask is, "Are there any waterfalls you can see from the road?" When they discover that Sequoia has neither a tree you can drive through, nor a waterfall you can see from the road, their third question is, "How far is it to Yosemite?"

While it's certainly true that Yosemite has some photogenic sights visible from the road, many people are beginning to realize that a little farther to the south, Sequoia has sights that even Yosemite can't match, along with a lot more peace and quiet. (Annual visitation at Sequoia and Kings Canyon is about 2.5 million, or roughly half that of Yosemite.) But to see Sequoia's finest sights, you have to get out of your car, put on a comfortable pair of shoes, and walk. Sequoia is a hiker's park. In fact, for the day hiker no park in the country offers more spectacular scenery than Sequoia. Giant Forest alone has more than fifty miles of hiking trails through its enchanting sequoia groves. Lodgepole has the waterfalls and granite cliffs the southern Sierra are so famous for. Mineral King has more than a dozen trails of startling alpine beauty. And the foothills, too often ignored by park visitors, are full of hidden groves, and lush rivers and creeks.

More people are visiting Sequoia than ever before—and not just Americans. You're almost as likely to hear German, French or Spanish spoken in the campgrounds these days as you are English. Oddly though, backcountry use in Sequoia is down from what it was in the Seventies and Eighties when the babyboomer generation flocked to the wilderness. This is probably because the babyboomers now have families and jobs, and they can't find the time for extended backpacking trips. But just as the sport of backpacking saw a huge surge in popularity during the 1960s and '70s, day hiking is seeing a wave of popularity today. Many of the babyboomers now take shorter day hikes as a way to share their love for the outdoors with their children.

An even bigger reason for the growing popularity of day hiking, though, is that there are more people interested in physical fitness than there were twenty-five years ago. In the 1960s, people drove their cars to the corner grocery store, believing the quarter-mile walk was beyond the range of human endurance. Nowadays there are millions of joggers competing in marathons and 10K races every weekend, and walking clubs are springing up all over the country.

It's only natural that fitness joggers and walkers would discover an interest in hiking. For those who jog the same urban routes day after day, hiking in a national park becomes a sensual delight. For runners who have injured their knees, Achilles tendons or shins, mild hiking can be a soothing relief. And for those fitness buffs looking for a challenge, pushing yourself up a steep trail at an elevation of 8000 feet can be a serious test of your fitness level.

But day hiking isn't just for the fitness fanatic or the experienced wilderness adventurer. It's a healthy form of recreation which all people can enjoy, regardless of their age, experience or physical condition. For those hikers hoping for an easy stroll, any trail in this guidebook could be described as easy if you go slowly enough and choose a reasonable stopping point. Almost all the trails in this guidebook are very well marked, and the exceptions are noted.

For those energetic hikers looking for challenge and adventure, many of the trail descriptions in this guidebook suggest interesting detours and alternate return routes. This guidebook lists virtually every possible day hike on a maintained trail in Sequoia, and by combining these trails with your own cross-country routes, the combinations for the experienced hiker are almost endless.

Still, you'll never see all of Sequoia and Kings Canyon with day hikes. That's one of the wonderful things about these parks: you can spend a lifetime exploring them.

So just how big is Sequoia? Although this guidebook deals only with Sequoia, in fact Sequoia and Kings Canyon are contiguous and are managed as one park. But the boundaries of the two parks are only bureaucratic formalities. It's more accurate to think of Sequoia as part of a much larger block of wilderness which includes the Sequoia, Kings Canyon, Inyo, Golden Trout, South Sierra, Domeland, Jenny Lakes, Monarch, John Muir, Dinkey, Kaiser, Ansel Adams and Yosemite wilderness areas. Together these make up one of the largest blocks of wilderness in the lower forty-eight states, extending 150 miles down the backbone of the Sierra Nevada.

Sequoia National Park has 402, 482 acres, over ninety percent of it wilderness. If Sequoia were broken into square-mile blocks, the fifty trails in this guidebook would touch perhaps ten percent of them. Combining all the views visible from all fifty trails, you would see perhaps twenty-five percent of Sequoia.

Any block of land as large and undeveloped as Sequoia will have a fascinating history and an intriguing flora and fauna. Part of the joy of exploring these lands is unraveling the natural mysteries and trying to understand the people and events that preceded us. In this guidebook I've briefly described a few historical events, identified a few plants and trees, and listed a few animals. But it would take a whole library of books to even begin to describe the complexity of a place like Sequoia. While you're in Sequoia, be sure to stop at one of the park service visitor centers and browse through the excellent books and pamphlets available there.

HOW TO USE THIS GUIDEBOOK

At the beginning of each trail description, the distance to one or more destinations is given, and it is specified whether these distances are one-way, or for a loop trail.

Also at the beginning of each trail description is an estimated time to complete the hike. These estimates are quite generous and allow for time to rest, to enjoy the sights, or to simply dawdle along. Fit and experienced hikers will often find they can complete the hike in half the suggested time if they choose to do so. Even average hikers will sometimes find they can complete the hike in less time than suggested. But hiking in a national park isn't the same as walking around the block at home, and more often than not you will want to spend more time completing the hike than is strictly necessary.

Each trail is rated for difficulty: Easy, Moderate, and Strenuous. Of course these are subjective judgments, and not all hikers will agree with the rating for any particular trail. Somebody hiking with twenty pounds of squirming child flesh on their back, or somebody hiking with twenty pounds of dead weight on their gut, may find that a trail rated as moderate is really quite difficult. On the other hand, somebody who has recently completed a fifty-mile backpacking trip will most likely find any trail described in this guidebook as being ridiculously easy. You can make your own estimate of each trail's difficulty by studying the map which accompanies each trail description, the total mileage given, and the total elevation gain or loss.

Although each hike in this guidebook has an accurate and updated topographic map to accompany it, the correct United States Geological Survey (USGS) map is also indicated for each hike. The recommended USGS maps are all 15 minute series. (The series simply describes the scale of the map.) Note that some 7.5 minute series maps have the same names as the 15-minute series maps (for example, Triple Divide), though they don't cover exactly the same area. To avoid confusion, if you choose to buy a separate USGS map, get the 15 minute series maps. It's optional to buy the USGS maps, but if you do buy them keep in mind that while the topographic detail on those maps is generally very accurate, some of the maps haven't been updated since 1956. Several of the trails shown on those maps are no longer in existence, and new trails have been added since the USGS maps were last updated. Also, the place names in this guidebook are more accurate than the USGS maps. Nevertheless, sometimes the only way to identify distant landmarks is by using the larger USGS maps. Perhaps the best method for those unfamiliar with Sequoia is to use both the USGS maps and the maps and descriptions in this guidebook. There are only four USGS 15-minute series quadrangles required for all the trails in this guidebook: Mineral King, Giant Forest, Triple Divide and Kaweah. The Kaweah quadrangle is out of print and nearly impossible to find. The Park Service also sells excellent detailed maps of the areas surrounding Giant Forest, Lodgepole and Mineral King. They only cost about $1.50 and can be purchased at any visitor center. There is also a USGS topographic map for all of Sequoia and Kings Canyon National Parks, but its scale is not always useful for day hiking.

Please note that the maps in this guidebook are intended to be a compromise between easy-to-read features for the novice hiker, and topographic accuracy for the experienced hiker. As with all maps, they are only a stylized representation of the physical world. Never trust a map more than you trust your own common sense.

Within each trail description, the major destinations along the route are noted, along with the mileage to that point and the approximate elevation. Notice that all distances given in the text are cumulative— that is, they are the total distance from the trailhead to that point.

At the entrance stations to the park, visitors are given a road map to Sequoia and Kings Canyon. Be sure to keep that map. While its scale is not suitable for hiking, it will be your best guide for finding your way around the roads of Sequoia and Kings Canyon and for finding the trailheads. At the beginning of each trail description you will find a place name (Hospital Rock, Crescent Meadow, etc.), which you will also find on the park's free map. After you have driven to that point, the description in this guidebook will lead you to the trailhead.

At the entrance stations, visitors are also given a copy of the park's newspaper. It will list the facilities and services available for each area of the park, the campgrounds, picnic areas, and so on. For more information on campgrounds and lodging accommodations, see Appendix 8 at the back of this guidebook.

You may notice some small discrepancies between distances given on trail signs and the distances given in this guidebook. These discrepancies occur because there is no foolproof method for measuring or estimating trail distances. While tenth-miles (for example, "Big Springs - 1.3 Miles") may give the impression of accuracy, in most cases that accuracy is only an illusion. For hiking purposes, quarter miles are as accurate as one can hope for. For example, a trail sign reading "Big Springs 1 1/4 Miles," is probably as accurate as a sign reading "Big Springs 1.3 Miles."

For the most part, you will find the trails described in this guidebook to be in good condition. The Park Service has four trail crews working in Sequoia, and each year every maintained trail is walked at least once by one of the crews. The trails are well marked, and even novice hikers should have no trouble following them. The occasional exceptions are noted in the descriptions.

To avoid confusion, all non-maintained routes in this guidebook will be referred to as footpaths, as in "a fisherman's footpath." The word "trail," on the other hand, will refer to those routes which receive routine maintenance.

You will find several references in this guidebook to the "North Fork," "South Fork," "Marble Fork," and so on. These all refer to forks of the Kaweah River, the only river you will encounter on front-country trails in Sequoia.

Some trail descriptions in this guidebook suggest cross-country routes for experienced hikers. If you aren't an experienced cross-country route finder, or you aren't in the company of an experienced route finder, don't try to follow these descriptions.

Every effort has been made to record the most accurate and up-to-date information available for each trail. Obviously, though, conditions will change. If you would like to contribute information or suggestions for future editions of this guidebook, write the author at P.O. Box 720, Three Rivers, CA 93271.

A FEW PRECAUTIONS TO KEEP IN MIND WHILE HIKING IN SEQUOIA

The terrain of the Sierra Nevada is as rugged as any mountain range on earth. With few exceptions the landscape is steep and rocky, and even on well-maintained trails hikers must spend considerable effort getting from one point to another. As the old saying goes, "In these mountains trails are uphill both ways." Besides the rugged terrain, you're coping with the high altitude, which is draining your body of perhaps one fourth of its efficiency. The remedy for both rough terrain and high altitude is to go a little slower. For most hikers it will take years to see all the trails in just the front-country of Sequoia and Kings Canyon, so take your time and enjoy them one by one.

In terms of climate, the Sierra Nevada is one of the gentlest mountain ranges on earth. John Muir often went into the backcountry for weeks at a time with nothing but a coat, a pocket knife, and a loaf of bread. Still, even in the summer the weather can change quickly. A morning that starts out warm and sunny can be cold and snowy by afternoon. Day hikers aren't exposed to these dangers as much as backcountry travelers, but you should still be prepared for anything. If, for example, a member of your party were to twist his ankle, you could find yourself having to return in the darkness. In an extreme emergency, you may even have to spend a night on the trail. Though most hikers can spend a lifetime in these parks without ever experiencing a serious accident or injury, you must always plan for the worst. Therefore, each member of your party should have a warm jacket or sweater, and at least some rain protection. A plastic trash bag with a hole cut out for the head makes a satisfactory rain coat. You should also have matches or lighter, a small first-aid kit, and above all, plenty of water.

You should know that hikers in Sequoia National Park have been injured and killed by lightning. In most cases, the hikers failed to take simple precautions to protect themselves. If any of the following conditions are present, find cover immediately: dark clouds nearby, lightning, hail, rain, hissing in the air, or static electricity in the hair or fingertips. Lightning-struck trees can shatter or even explode. Large overhanging boulders often provide the best shelter.

If you are hiking below 5000 feet, there's a good chance you will see poison oak. In most places, though, it has been pruned away from the trail. If you aren't familiar with this troublesome plant, look for a shrub with shiny leaves in groups of three, and white berries. If you should develop a rash shortly after a hike, be sure to wash your clothes in hot water before wearing them again, and wash your skin with soap and hot water. There is really very little else you can do for poison-oak rash, except wait for the rash to go away. A hot shower, followed by an application of hydro-cortisone cream will help relieve the itching.

If you are hiking in the lower foothills of the park, you could encounter ticks, particularly in brushy areas, and particularly during the winter and spring when ticks are more numerous. Stay on the trails and avoid contact with brush if possible. If you're hiking with someone else, periodically check each other's hair, neck, arms and clothing. (If you have never seen a tick before, they're brown or black, about the size of a pinhead.) Pay careful attention to any itching on your skin; usually you can feel a tick trying to burrow into your skin before it becomes fully attached. If a tick does become attached, do not put anything on its body such as alcohol or a hot match. Carefully remove the tick with a pair of tweezers, grasping it as closely to your skin as possible. Do not try to remove the tick with your fingers—you'll only mash its body, leaving the head embedded in your skin.

In recent years there has been a lot of media attention on Lyme disease, a potentially serious illness caused by a spirochete transmitted by a tick bite. This media attention has reached nearly hysterical proportions, but for the careful and alert hiker, the danger of acquiring Lyme disease from a tick bite in this region of California is very small. Of the many types of ticks, only one, the black-legged tick, carries the disease. Of black-legged ticks, only a very small percentage actually have the spirochete in their bodies. Furthermore, the tick must be attached to your skin for several hours before it is able to transmit the spirochete. (Some doctors now say the tick must be attached for at least thirty-six hours before the spirochete can be transmitted.) If you will examine your skin after hiking in brushy areas, you can reduce your chances of acquiring the disease to virtually zero.

You could come across black bears on any trail in the park. Black bears are far less dangerous than their cousins, the grizzlies, which have not been found in this park since the 1920s. The only real dangers with black bears are if you are feeding them, or if you should accidentally come between a mother and its cubs. Remember, do not feed the bears. If you see an adult bear, look around for any cubs, and keep your distance from them. Also, if you encounter a bear on a trail surrounded by thick brush, the bear can possibly feel it has been cornered and charge toward you in search of a way out. You should always give a bear an escape route. If a bear is making a persistent effort to get food from you, shout, make loud noises, and throw small rocks toward it. Most black bears can be easily chased away.

Almost every year someone drowns in one of the park's many rivers or creeks. Often these victims were diving from the cliffs, swimming in rapids, swimming while intoxicated, or otherwise taking risks a cautious person would not take. But there is also the danger of the uninformed visitor misjudging the swiftness of the current, the steepness of the rocky banks, or the coldness of the water. Remember that any time you are near a river or creek there is a potential danger. Keep young children away at all times. Most of the trails in this guidebook have safe bridges at major river and creek crossings, but in the spring and early summer even small creeks can be swollen and dangerous. Always use extreme caution near rivers and creeks.

Rattlesnakes in this park are most common in areas below 8000 feet. If you will be hiking in the foothills, you should consider carrying a snake bite kit. (Not one of the old rubber suction types, which are useless, but the newer syringe types.) Though rattlesnake bites aren't nearly as common, nor as dangerous, as many people think (far more people in the United States die of bee stings every year than snakebites), it's still not a bad idea to carry a snakebite kit and to know how to use it. Though hikers could happen upon a rattlesnake at any time, the danger of being bitten is not great. Keep in mind that normally a coiled snake can only strike about half its length; since almost all rattlesnakes in this area are less than four feet long, to avoid being bitten you need to always watch at least two feet in front of you. Also, rattlesnakes can't tolerate intense sunlight for more than a few minutes and they become quite sluggish in cool temperatures. For these reasons, rattlesnakes are most often seen in the late afternoon and evening. If you're in the foothills, be particularly alert for rattlesnakes at that time of day.

Most snakebites occur because the victim was teasing, touching, or trying to kill the snake. Your best precaution with rattlesnakes is to leave them alone. In the unlikely event that you are bitten by a snake, keep in mind that in a very high percentage of cases, venom is not injected by the snake. Even if venom is injected, rattlesnake bites on the extremities are rarely fatal. So there is no reason to panic. As with any injury, remain calm and seek help from the nearest park rangers.

Although the water in the park's rivers and creeks certainly appears to be clear and inviting to a thirsty hiker, you should not drink it. All surface water in the park should be considered contaminated with Giardia, a microscopic parasite which can cause diarrhea and other intestinal problems. Water filters are available at backpacking stores, but their usefulness in filtering Giardia cysts is uncertain. Boiling the water is very effective in killing the cysts, though not very practical for day hikers. The best solution is to carry a water bottle or canteen with water from the campgrounds, or from some other treated water source.

It's easy to underestimate the amount of water you will need to carry on a day hike. The Sierra Nevada is often cool in the summer, but the air is also very dry. You're working hard while hiking, and it's easy to become dehydrated. For a four-hour hike, you should carry at least two quarts of water per person.

As for food, keep in mind that hiking at high altitude requires at least as much energy as jogging at sea level. If you pass by one of the pack stations in the early morning, you may notice that the horses and mules are each being given a nose bag of grain. Likewise, you should load up on carbohydrates before a strenuous hike. Candy and sweets may give you a burst of energy, but they will soon leave you feeling tired. Bread, cereals, nuts and granola have long been traditional hiking fare, and for good reason.

Keep in mind that although hiking uphill may seem to require more effort, hiking downhill is often harder on your body. Your ankles, knees and hips take a battering going downhill, and injuries are much more common: slips, falls, twisted ankles, and so on. You should make a conscious effort while going downhill to control your speed and to watch your footing carefully. Though this requires concentration, at the end of the day your body will feel the difference.

If you're hiking with children younger than two years old, you're probably going to end up carrying them part of the way. Pound for pound, young children are more useful than anything else you might carry on your back. It's nice to have somebody looking over your shoulder, keeping you company, and offering criticism of the route you have chosen. But if you don't plan on carrying your young children, keep your hikes short. Appendix 4 lists trails in each area which are suitable for young children.

For children between two and eight, remember to let them set their own pace. They will become easily distracted by all the curiosities along the way, but if you try to hurry them along you will only make the experience frustrating for both of you. Trail hiking is a learned pleasure. Start children out slowly, and they will soon learn to enjoy hiking as much as you do.

When hiking with children older than eight, *you* may end up being the slow one. Teen-agers, especially, may want to charge on ahead. But remember that everyone in your party should stay within sight of the person who is carrying the guidebook and map. There will be many junctions along these trails, and probably the easiest way for someone to get lost or separated is by hiking too far ahead of the rest of the party.

Every time you start out on a hike, it's a good idea to pause for a moment and think, Where is the nearest telephone, where is the nearest ranger station, and where would I go for help if an emergency did occur? From any telephone in the park you can dial 911 to report an emergency; no coin is necessary. The Park Service has several paramedics who can respond quickly to nearly any location described in this text.

Please remember not to cut switchbacks while hiking these trails. Not only is it dangerous, but cutting switchbacks makes the trail maintenance crews' job more difficult, and it causes soil erosion which can lead to very serious damage to the park resources. It just takes a few moments more to follow the trail.

Most of all, remember that the whole point of hiking is your enjoyment. If you aren't enjoying your hike, it's probably because you're trying to go too fast. Regardless of your physical condition, go slowly enough to make your experience an enjoyable one.

Sequoia Cone

South Fork of the Kaweah near Ladybug

Introduction to the Foothills

Most visitors to Sequoia don't pay much attention to the foothills. From the road these areas appear hot, steep, rocky and brushy. But for those who are willing to look a bit closer, the foothills contain pockets of paradise which, in some ways, are more accommodating to the human visitor than any other area of the park. The Indians who once lived in the park made all of their permanent villages in the foothills, where the winters are generally as sunny and pleasant as anywhere in California and there's a greater variety of plant and animal life than can be found at higher elevations. Some animals, like the deer and bear, spend their summers in the high country but migrate to the lower elevations as soon as the cold weather arrives.

The term "foothills" is not a precise one; for the purposes of this guidebook it's used to describe those lower-elevation areas on the western side of the park. Usually the foothills are below the conifers, in the oak- and chaparral-covered regions of the park, though you will also find that several of the foothill trails begin in the chaparral and oaks but soon lead you into the mid-elevation areas where you find pines, firs and even giant sequoias. Generally speaking, these foothill areas are at their best during the fall, winter and spring, but they can be enjoyed during the summer too by hiking during the early morning hours or during the cool evenings.

You'll find that almost all of the trails described in this section pass near a river or creek. In some ways these riparian areas are what make the foothills so attractive. Their pools are not only beautiful to look at and sensuous to swim in, but they provide a lush ribbon of landscape in what would otherwise be an arid semi-desert.

Some of the rivers and creeks offer good fishing and are likely places to spot wildlife, but they can also be very dangerous. Those who have never been swimming in an icy river would not believe how quickly the cold water can cramp your muscles and drain your strength. Even powerful swimmers can easily underestimate the strength of the current. Swimming in the park's rivers should only be done with extreme caution, especially in the spring and early summer when the water level is high.

Note also that in late summer the rivers tend to accumulate a lot of pollen, particularly from the pines, oaks and grasses. If you have a fit of hay fever after swimming in one of the rivers, pollen is probably the cause. Many people, however, are not affected.

Much of the foothills area is steep, and the rock, which consists of slate, schist and marble, is often loose and crumbly. These areas are not safe for climbing, especially when compared to the higher elevation areas where firm granite is much more common. People used to living in an urban environment, where even the slightest hazard is marked with a yellow caution sign, sometimes fail to accurately judge the risk involved when climbing on these steep, rocky, foothill slopes. Unless you're an experienced climber, or in the company of an experienced climber, stay on the trails.

Other dangers worth noting while hiking in the foothills include rattlesnakes, poison oak and ticks. If you're unfamiliar with these, look to the introduction of this guidebook for more information about their hazards.

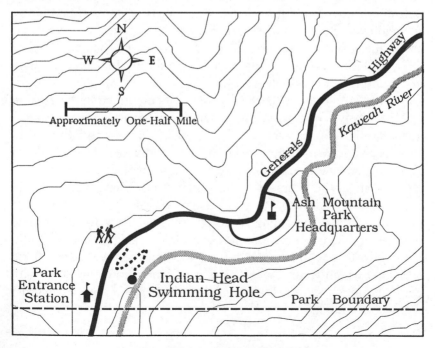

Indian Head Swimming Hole

THE INDIAN HEAD SWIMMING HOLE

DISTANCE: 1/4 Mile
HIKING TIME: 10 Minutes
STARTING ELEVATION: 1500'
LOWEST ELEVATION: 1400'
DIFFICULTY: Easy
USGS MAP: Kaweah

If you've spent several hours driving to the park, this is an opportunity to stretch your legs and cool off—the perfect refreshment on a hot summer day.

From the Ash Mountain entrance station, on Highway 198, proceed up the road 0.1 miles. Look for the parking lot, on the right side of the highway, with a large carved Indian head. The trail begins on the south side of the parking area and is marked with a trail sign.

Almost as soon as you start down the trail you can see the large, emerald-green pools below. Looking upstream you can see Moro Rock and Alta Peak. There is some poison oak along the trailside here. (Look for shiny leaves in clusters of three.) If you can't identify poison oak, don't touch any foliage.

Just three short switchbacks bring you to the Middle Fork of the Kaweah and the Indian Head Swimming Hole. The largest of the pools is longer and deeper than an Olympic-sized swimming pool, and there are smaller pools upstream. The pools are generally safe in late summer, when the water is calm, but use extreme caution in the spring and early summer when the water level is high and the current swift. There are also several flat, water-polished rocks for lying in the sun.

The Kaweah is one of four major rivers in Sequoia and Kings Canyon National Parks, the others being the Kern, the Kings and the San Joaquin. The word "Kaweah" is a Yokuts name and is said to mean something like "raven's call." It's a good name. Ravens are particularly fond of the southern Sierra and can often be heard flapping and squawking along the Kaweah's many forks.

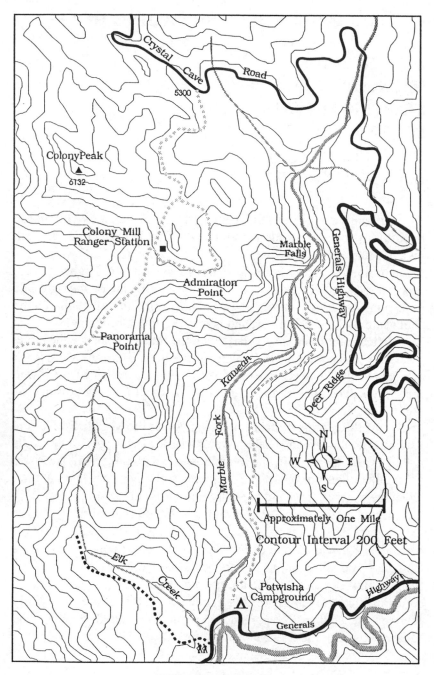

Elk Creek Trail

ELK CREEK TRAIL

DISTANCE: 1 Mile (one way)
HIKING TIME: 30 Minutes (one way)
STARTING ELEVATION: 2000'
HIGHEST ELEVATION: 2500'
DIFFICULTY: Easy
USGS MAP: Giant Forest

Except for the early morning hours, this seldom-used trail will probably be too hot for summer hiking. But during the spring and fall it can be pleasant, and during the winter the southern exposure makes it a sunny and enjoyable hike.

At one time this trail continued all the way to the Colony Mill Road, but the thick chamise makes the trail difficult to maintain and now it's only clear for about the first mile.

On the Generals Highway, 3.6 miles east of the Ash Mountain entrance station, and 0.2 miles west of Potwisha Campground, look for a small parking area on the west side of the road. There is no sign marking the trailhead here, so you have to look carefully to find it.

The trail follows a dry creek bed for just one hundred feet, then turns west. For the first 1/4 mile you follow a route under the power lines, sometimes within sight of the highway. Then, on a grassy, oak-covered knoll, the trail finally turns north and heads uphill.

By 1/2 mile you've gained enough elevation to have a good view of Moro Rock, Castle Rocks to the south, and Mt. Stewart to the distant east. The rocky knoll to the north is Panorama Point.

According to Hale Tharp, the first white settler in this area, there were no elk in the foothills when he arrived here in 1856, so the name Elk Creek is a bit of a mystery. Tule elk were quite common in the San Joaquin Valley, however, and in the early part of this century the Park Service experimented unsuccessfully with relocating them in Sequoia. Because of the great popularity of Yellowstone National Park, it was believed that any respectable mountain park should have at least some elk, just as any hiker should wear riding breeches, knee-high leggings and a hat that looked as if it had seen the Spanish-American War. The trouble was, elk are primarily a grass and woodlands animal ill-suited for the hot, rugged slopes of Elk Creek. At any rate, perhaps this creek's name dates back to that failed experiment.

You now pass through thick stands of chamise that are sometimes head high. The Park Service is committed to a program of prescribed burning that will thin brush lands like this in order to improve animal habitat and reduce the danger of destructive wildfires. As you can see, that job will be a big one.

At 1 mile the chamise becomes impenetrable to all but reptiles and small rodents. Larger creatures would be wise to turn back at this point.

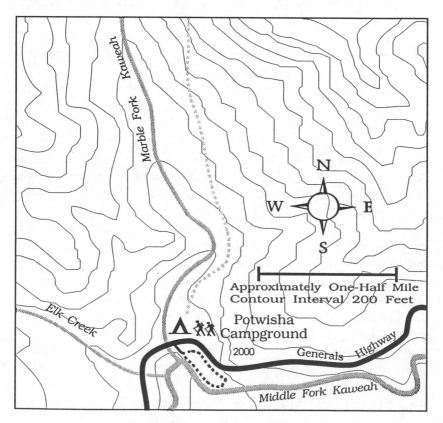

Potwisha Pictographs Loop

POTWISHA PICTOGRAPHS LOOP

DISTANCE: 1/2 Mile
HIKING TIME: 30 Minutes
STARTING ELEVATION: 2000'
HIGHEST ELEVATION: 2100'
DIFFICULTY: Easy
USGS MAP: Giant Forest

This interesting little loop takes you by Indian bedrock mortars, pictographs and a couple of good, medium-size swimming holes.

On the Generals Highway, 3.8 miles east of the Ash Mountain entrance station, you come to Potwisha campground. Directly across the highway from the entrance to the campground is a paved road which leads south 0.1 miles to an RV dump station. Take that paved road and continue to the right (west) another 0.1 miles to the end of the road and the trailhead.

Follow the trail south through the boulders for 200 feet, where you will begin to see bedrock mortars just above the Middle Fork of the Kaweah.

This area was once part of an Indian village site known as Potwisha, occupied by a group of Monaches. The main part of the village was probably about where the RV dump station is now. Standing in the middle of the bedrock mortars and looking south about one hundred feet, you see an overhanging rock; a manzanita and several buckeyes grow above the rock. If you look carefully on the underside of the rock, you can see several pictographs.

In recent years it has been learned that many ancient pictographs around California, and elsewhere in the West, were used by Indian shamans to predict winter and summer solstices. The rock drawings marked light patterns which only appeared during the time of the solstices. But pictographs like this one at Potwisha fall into a different category, and are often found near bedrock mortars. Because the mortars were used to grind acorns, and because only women ground acorns, these kinds of pictographs are associated with women. Yet no one knows what meaning these drawings had for the Indian women. Perhaps the drawings were used to help recount tribal tales for the amusement and instruction of their children during the long and tedious chore of grinding acorns.

There are some good swimming holes near this site, and you can be sure the people of Potwisha used them often. The Indians of central California were water lovers. Even in the winter, the entire village began the day with a dip in the river, and the people returned to the water to bathe several times throughout the day.

The trail continues now just above the river, and you soon come to a sandy beach on a ledge just above another good swimming hole. Beyond that you find a suspension bridge above the river. This bridge gives access to Southern California Edison Company's flume, which follows the south side of the river. Fishermen also find the bridge useful.

This trail does not cross the bridge; it turns east (upstream), then north, and climbs a steep but short hill.

Near the top of the hill, and just short of the highway, you come to the Middle Fork Trail. Turn left (west), and follow it a short way to the parking area.

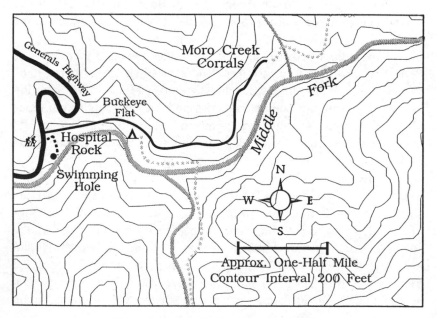

Hospital Rock Swimming Hole

HOSPITAL ROCK SWIMMING HOLE

DISTANCE: 1/8 Mile
HIKING TIME: 5 Minutes
STARTING ELEVATION: 2800'
LOWEST ELEVATION: 2700'
DIFFICULTY: Easy
USGS MAP: Giant Forest

Beginning at the Hospital Rock parking area, walk across the Generals Highway to the Indian exhibit. Here you find some of the finest examples of Indian pictographs in the park. There are also bedrock mortar holes that were used by the Indians for grinding acorns. Hospital Rock was once the largest Indian village within the boundaries of the park. Unfortunately, most of the site is now covered by the parking lot.

Hale Tharp, the first white settler in this area, was brought to Hospital Rock by a band of Indians in 1858. He described the village, which contained about 600 people, as the cleanest he had ever seen, and described the people as honest and kind.

Oddly, the Indians asked Tharp if he would explain to them the meaning of the pictographs drawn on the walls of the boulder caves. The Indians said the drawings had been there for as long as any of their people could recall, and they had no knowledge of their meaning. A possible explanation for this is that the people of Hospital Rock were Monaches, cultural and linguistic relatives of the Owens Valley Paiutes on the eastern side of the Sierra, while the people farther down the river were mostly Yokuts, a completely different language family; for centuries the Monaches had been encroaching upon what had traditionally been Yokuts territory. Though the two groups were not exactly enemies, they were rivals and had some mistrust for each other. Perhaps Hospital Rock had once been a Yokuts village, and because the pictographs had been part of their cultural life, they refused to explain the meaning of the drawings to the Monaches.

At the time of Hale Tharp's arrival, the boulder cave was being used as a shelter for two Indian women, one with a broken leg and one who was nursing a baby. Traditionally, the cave had been used by the village medicine man as a place to treat the sick and injured. Hale Tharp gave the place the name of Hospital Rock. Later, in 1873, a white settler, Alfred Everton, suffered a gunshot wound to the leg and was carried to the boulder caves to rest until a doctor could be brought from Visalia. That incident reinforced the name of Hospital Rock.

Just south of the Indian exhibit is a paved trail which leads from the Generals Highway down to the Middle Fork of the Kaweah, where you will find several large pools.

It's no accident that nearly all Indian village sites in the park are located near a good swimming hole. California Indians loved the water. They were expert swimmers, and even in the winter began every day with a bath at dawn.

Some early accounts described the California Indians as being dirty. Even the great conservationist, John Muir, contributed to this misconception. In one book he writes of Miwoks he encountered in the summer of 1869: "A strangely dirty and irregular life these dark-eyed, dark-haired, half-happy savages lead in this clean wilderness...." At another point he writes, "The dirt on some of the faces seemed almost old enough and thick enough to have a geological significance."

What Muir failed to understand was that when California Indians were in mourning, they refused to wash their faces; in fact, they caked their faces with pitch and ashes to demonstrate their extreme sorrow at the loss of a loved one. At the time Muir visited the Sierra, the Indian population had been decimated by smallpox and other diseases brought to them by gold diggers and by sheepherders like John Muir. Most likely all the Indians seen by Muir, and other early visitors to these mountains, were in mourning.

Under normal circumstances, California Indians bathed themselves several times throughout the day; when the first whites arrived, wearing their heavy woolen clothing even in summer and almost never bathing, the Indians considered them smelly beyond toleration.

So take off your long johns and wash away the smell of civilization, keeping in mind that these pools below Hospital Rock were enjoyed by many generations before you.

Pictographs at Hospital Rock

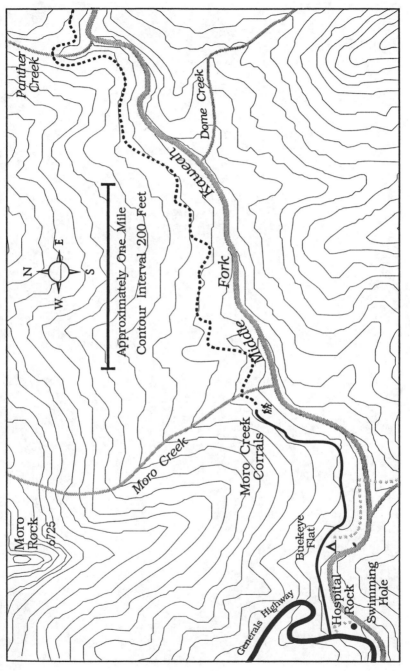

Middle Fork Trail

MIDDLE FORK TRAIL

Moro Creek Corrals to Panther Creek

DISTANCE: 3 Miles (one way)
HIKING TIME: 2 Hours (one way)
STARTING ELEVATION: 3350'
HIGHEST ELEVATION: 3900'
DIFFICULTY: Moderate
USGS MAPS: Giant Forest and Triple Divide

This trail offers a dizzying view from the top of a waterfall on Panther Creek, as well as an interesting look at the effects of the Buckeye Fire of 1988.

The name "Middle Fork Trail" can be a bit confusing. A non-maintained trail, mostly used for stock travel, begins at the Ash Mountain Corrals and follows above and below the Generals Highway for 5.5 miles to Hospital Rock. That portion of the Middle Fork Trail isn't particularly scenic and therefore isn't described here as suitable for day hiking.

To hike the more interesting upper portion of the Middle Fork Trail, begin at the Hospital Rock parking area and walk or drive east on the Buckeye Flat Road. (During the summer months you can drive the 1.8 miles from Hospital Rock to Moro Creek Corrals; in the winter the gate is locked at Hospital Rock.) At 0.5 miles you come to a dirt road marked by a wooden sign which reads, "Middle Fork Trail 1.3 Miles." Follow this road uphill to its end, at Moro Creek Corrals.

Here you begin to see the nearly disastrous effects of the Buckeye Fire of 1988. This wildfire was started by a carelessly discarded cigarette, and roared 3000 feet up the steep slopes, charring 3100 acres before it was finally stopped at Giant Forest.

Pass through the narrow gate, and in just 400 feet you come to Moro Creek, where you find a small grove of alders and willows.

The trail begins climbing moderately now and soon gives you a fine view of Moro Rock, to the northwest. From this vantage point it's easy to understand the Indian name for Moro Rock, which was "The Turtle's Back."

At 1/2 mile you come to a small, unnamed creek. In the days before there were any roads to Giant Forest, a trail used by the Indians and early settlers followed the ridge west of this creek and led to Crescent Meadow. In another 1/2 mile you will be able to look back and see a trace of that old trail.

Since the fire of 1988, the landscape along this first mile of trail has been going through some dramatic changes. While some plants such as live oak and manzanita were completely killed by the fire, others like chamise and laurel only lost their crowns and have re-sprouted from their charred stumps. Meanwhile, the seeds of manzanita, which could not get established in the thick brush before the fire, are now sprouting by the thousands.

At about 1 mile, you leave the area burned by the fire. Here you see the old, thick stands of chamise. Before the Buckeye Fire, old stands of brush such as this covered much of the Middle Fork. These old brush lands offer little in the way of food for larger animals, like deer, but the tender young sprouts of chamise and manzanita that appear after a fire are tender and nourishing. In that sense, the fire did some good by clearing the old brush. But the wildfire did its worst damage several thousand feet up the slope, where the conifers begin. Many large pines and firs were destroyed, and if the fire hadn't been stopped at the Crescent Meadow Road, it could have destroyed the groves of sequoias in Giant Forest.

By intentionally setting controlled fires, under prescribed conditions, the Park Service can achieve all the benefits of fire with few of the drawbacks. In this particular situation, the Park Service would have waited until the fall when burn conditions weren't so volatile, then they would have ignited a fire at the Crescent Meadow Road and allowed it to burn slowly down to the canyon floor. This kind of controlled burning isn't nearly as expensive as fighting wildfires.

As you continue up the Middle Fork Trail, you have several excellent views of the Great Western Divide to the east, and of Castle Rocks to the south.

At about 2 1/2 miles, you climb a few short, rocky switchbacks. Directly across the canyon is Dome Creek. Along its cool, north-facing slopes you begin to see several types of conifers. If you look carefully on the ridge to the southeast of Dome Creek you can see a few giant sequoias that are part of the Castle Creek Grove.

And 3 miles brings you to Panther Creek, where you have a very dramatic view of the creek cascading over a granite cliff and into the Kaweah River. The large clear pools, nearly 200 feet below, are very tempting but are impossible to reach without climbing equipment. There are several cool, flat places among the pines and cedars on Panther Creek where you can rest. There are also a few swimming holes here, but the banks are steep and rocky, so use caution.

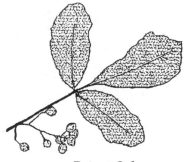

Poison Oak

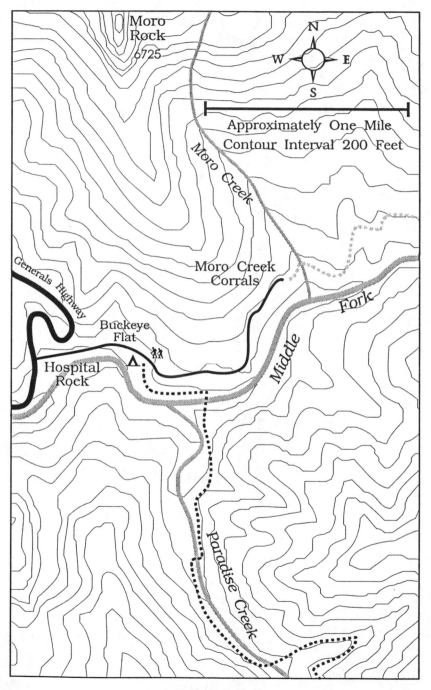

Paradise Creek Trail

PARADISE CREEK TRAIL

DISTANCE: 3 Miles (one way)
HIKING TIME: 2 Hours (one way)
STARTING ELEVATION: 2800'
HIGHEST ELEVATION: 4400'
DIFFICULTY: Moderate
USGS MAPS: Giant Forest, Triple Divide and Mineral King

This beautiful trail is one of the oldest trails in the park. In the 1870s, when silver ore was being mined in Mineral King and sequoias were being logged at Atwell Mill, the Paradise Creek Trail served as a shortcut from Mineral King to the Middle Fork of the Kaweah. Over the years, as the Mineral King Road was gradually improved, the Paradise Creek Trail fell out of use. Today only the first 3 miles of the trail are maintained. Note that although this trail is rated as moderate in difficulty, the first 1 1/2 miles are very gentle and are appropriate for children or less ambitious hikers.

Beginning at the Hospital Rock parking area, walk or drive along the paved road 0.6 miles to Buckeye Flat campground. In the summer you can drive to Buckeye Flat campground, but in the winter the gate is locked at Hospital Rock. Day-use parking is not allowed at Buckeye Flat campground, so unless you have somebody drop you off at the campground you must begin at Hospital Rock.

The trailhead for the Paradise Creek Trail is just one hundred feet south of the information sign as you enter Buckeye Flat campground.

The trail skirts the eastern edge of the campground and quickly brings you to the Middle Fork bridge. Cross the wooden bridge and in just 150 feet you see a small footpath branching from the main trail and leading to the right (west). This short detour takes you to a small waterfall and swimming hole on the lower end of Paradise Creek.

Continuing up the main trail, you pass through a grove of manzanita which includes a few specimens twenty-five feet high and twelve inches in diameter at the base. You soon discover that although the surrounding hillsides are rocky and brushy, the areas along the creek are lush with a wonderful variety of plant life: pines, cedars, sycamores, alders, laurels, black oaks, blue oaks and many more.

At 1/2 mile, looking back, you have a unique view of Moro Rock. From other vantage points Moro Rock appears to be a dome, but from here it's easy to see the rock is shaped more like the fin of a large fish.

The trail now closely follows the creek, and you pass several fine pools. At about 3/4 miles you cross Paradise Creek. This is generally a safe crossing, but use caution when the water level is high. At about 1 mile you cross back again to the east side.

At about 1 3/4 miles, and an elevation of 3600 feet, the trail begins climbing the steep southwest-facing slope, following a small but rugged drainage. You pass through a very dense grove of live oaks, with lush stands of ferns growing in the shade. The trail becomes narrow in places. At 2 miles you cross the small drainage.

By 2 1/4 miles you emerge from the dense grove of oaks and begin to have some fine views of the opposite side of Paradise Canyon. You cross an open rocky face where the trail becomes even more narrow. To the south you can now see Paradise Ridge where, more than a hundred years ago, this trail once led. You can decide for yourself at what point it is no longer practical to follow the trail.

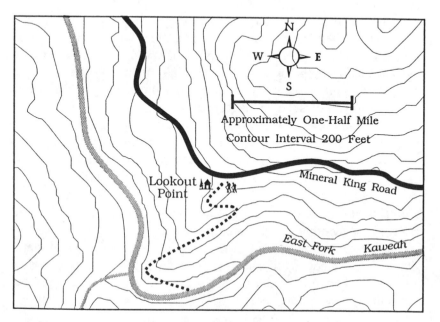

Lookout Point Trail

LOOKOUT POINT TRAIL

DISTANCE: 1/2 Mile (one way)
HIKING TIME: 30 Minutes (longer return trip)
STARTING ELEVATION: 4019′
LOWEST ELEVATION: 3450′
DIFFICULTY: Strenuous (return trip)
USGS MAP: Kaweah

This rugged and seldom-used trail is favored by the few fishermen who know of its existence. The trail is in an area of very thick chamise, and even though the park trail crews periodically prune the brush away from the trail, it quickly grows back, making the trail sometimes hard to follow.

Begin at the Lookout Point Ranger Station, on the Mineral King Road, 10.3 miles east of Highway 198. In front of the ranger station is an information sign. Park in front of the sign and walk east about twenty feet, where you find the trailhead.

As you start down the trail, look up canyon and you can see Sawtooth Peak, above Mineral King Valley. Across the canyon, to the south, you see Case Mountain, outside of Sequoia National Park but home to many giant sequoias.

The trail descends steeply through thick chamise. Ticks seem to favor chamise over all other vegetation, so be extra alert for these pests.

At about 1/4 mile, looking across the canyon, you may be able to see a faint trace of an old trail. At one time the trail you are now hiking continued beyond the East Fork, climbing the ridge above Coffeepot Canyon, to Case Mountain. As you can see, the brush has reclaimed most of that old route.

As you descend, the brush begins to thin somewhat and you soon hear the sound of the river. You enter a green belt of cedars, live oaks and laurels just before you reach the East Fork of the Kaweah. There's a small campsite here, as well as several shallow pools. It's possible to walk a short distance both upstream and downstream, but use extreme caution when the water level is high.

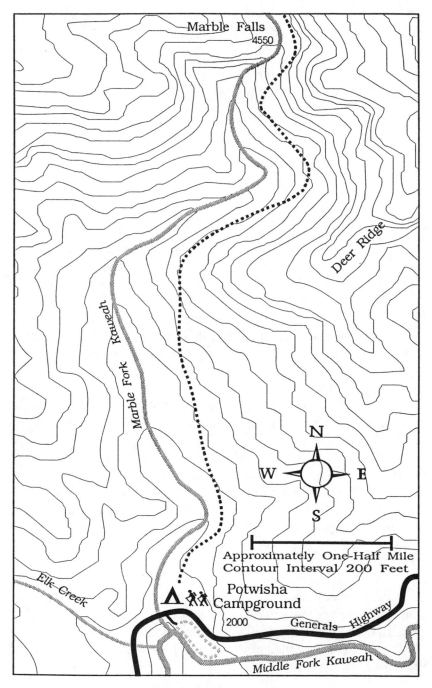

Marble Fork Trail

MARBLE FORK TRAIL

DISTANCE: 3 Miles (one way)
HIKING TIME: 2 Hours (one way)
STARTING ELEVATION: 2000'
HIGHEST ELEVATION: 4550'
DIFFICULTY: Strenuous
USGS MAP: Giant Forest

The Marble Fork Trail is one of the most dramatic foothill trails in the park, leading to a deep gorge with roaring waterfalls and multi-colored boulders. Because of the south- and west-facing slopes along this trail, it tends to be warm; in the winter this warmth is a pleasure, but if you're hiking in the summer be sure to get an early start.

The trail begins in Potwisha campground, located on the Generals Highway 3.8 miles east of the Ash Mountain entrance station. Drive to the north end of the campground, then look for the small parking area north of campsite 16.

Hike north on the graveled service road, following the Southern California Edison Company flume. After crossing the wooden bridge over the flume, you soon come to a wooden trail sign which reads, "Marble Fork Trail," and points east, uphill.

The trail climbs a few short but fairly steep switchbacks, passing by some impressive specimens of poison oak with diameters at the base of three to four inches. In the winter, after the leaves have fallen, these may be hard to identify. Look for the vine-like trunks spiraling up through the live oaks. The pale berries of the poison oak may still be present.

The trail's grade soon becomes more tolerable and maintains this moderate grade for the remainder of the hike. For the next couple of miles, the trail passes alternately through sunny slopes covered with chamise and cool drainages grown dense with spice bush, cottonwoods and sycamores.

The Marble Fork Trail is one of many in Sequoia built by the Civilian Conservation Corps during the Great Depression of the 1930s and early 40s. In fact most of the trail system in this park was either built or improved by the boys of the CCC working under the leadership of skilled trail foremen. This particular trail was completed by the CCC in 1938.

You pass by some large yuccas, with their pale-green, needle-tipped leaves. In the spring the yucca's spear-like flower stalks are tender and edible. The Indians baked yucca spears, almost like squash, but the spears are also delicious raw, and taste something like cucumber. Even the cream-colored flowers are edible; they taste a bit like artichokes.

At about 1 mile you gain a view to the north. A sharp pair of eyes can spot the approximate location of the Colony Mill Ranger Station, in a saddle on Ash Peaks Ridge. (See page 109.) Look for the red banks of the road leading up to the ranger station.

Looking back to the south you can see Milk Ranch Peak and perhaps even the fire lookout tower perched on it's bald knoll. Look for the windows glistening in the sun.

At 2 miles, and an elevation of 3200 feet, the trail rounds a point in the canyon and allows a clear view of the upper end of the gorge. Looking to the east you may be able to see part of the Generals Highway, some 2000 feet above.

You now pass through thick groves of California laurel, or bay. This is similar to the Mediterranean variety of bay sold in grocery stores as a spice for cooking, though this California variety is quite a bit more potent.

2 1/4 miles brings you to a rocky outcropping where you have a view of the bottom of the canyon. Here you see Marble Falls, not very high but very beautiful. Looking about 200 feet above the falls, you can see part of the trail.

The trail now passes through areas of white and gray marble. This belt of marble, which is found in several places throughout the foothills of the park, contains several caves (Crystal Cave, Clough Cave, Paradise Cave), though none are known to exist in this part of the Marble Fork.

By 2 3/4 miles you come to a cool creek flowing over marble slabs. Part of the trail has collapsed here; look for it beyond the creek and about twenty feet higher up the slope.

You pass through a grove of California nutmeg, a fairly uncommon tree in the southern Sierra. Its sharp, single needles make it look something like a fir.

And 3 miles brings you to the end of the trail, deep in the bottom of the gorge, beside the Marble Fork of the Kaweah.

It's almost impossible to hike farther up the canyon, and to venture down the river is very hazardous and should only be attempted by careful and experienced hikers. Use extreme caution here when the water level is high. The boulders and rocky slopes are exceptionally slippery and treacherous. The marble and slate found here are not suitable for rock climbing, they break very easily and have led to many injuries in the park. Do not climb in this area.

California Nutmeg

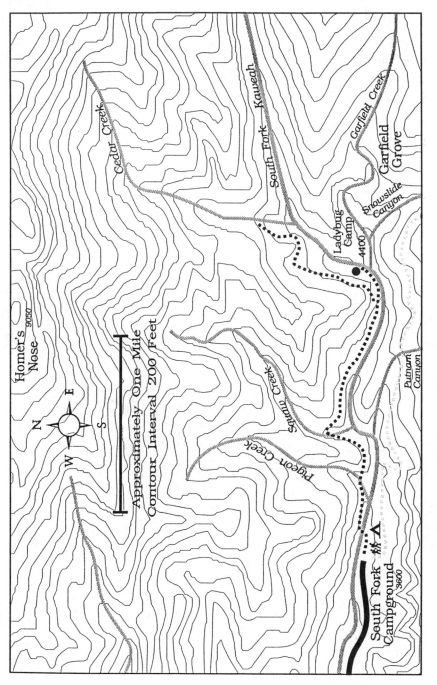

Ladybug Trail

LADYBUG TRAIL

DISTANCE: 3 Miles (to Cedar Creek)
HIKING TIME: 2 Hours (one way)
STARTING ELEVATION: 3600'
HIGHEST ELEVATION: 5000'
DIFFICULTY: Moderate
USGS MAPS: Kaweah and Mineral King

Of all the foothill trails in the park, the Ladybug Trail is the most beautiful. In the summer it offers opportunities for swimming and fishing along the South Fork of the Kaweah, and in the winter its south-facing slopes offer sunny warmth. Except for the Garfield-Hockett Trail, it is the only day hike in the foothills which takes you to giant sequoias.

The Ladybug Trail begins at South Fork campground. From Highway 198 in Three Rivers, follow South Fork Drive about 13 miles to the park entrance and campground. (See the map on page 10.) To find South Fork Drive on Highway 198, look for the fire station on the south side of the road about one mile east of Three Rivers Post Office.

There is no entrance fee or day-use fee at South Fork campground. Park at the day-use parking area at the entrance, then walk up the dirt road, through the campground. A brown sign marking the trailhead reads, "Ladybug Trail."

The trail follows the river for 300 feet, then crosses the South Fork of the Kaweah on a wooden foot bridge. After a short but steep climb, the trail turns east. It then follows above the river, climbing moderately while passing through dense groves of live oaks, nutmegs and laurels.

At 1/2 mile you cross Pigeon Creek, often dry in the summer. A non-maintained footpath, difficult to follow, climbs the ridge just west of this creek to Case Mountain.

Continuing up the trail, you soon have views of pine-covered Dennison Ridge to the south. At 3/4 miles, where the river makes a bend to the north, you have a view across the canyon of a waterfall on Putnam Creek.

1 mile brings you to Squaw Creek, where there's a pleasant place to rest in an alder grove.

At about 1 1/4 miles you begin to see several footpaths leading down to the river. Some of these are fairly steep, so use them only with caution. A sharp eye will spot a few sequoias growing along the river here. These sequoias are the lowest in elevation of any naturally-occurring sequoias in the world. It has been speculated that they were carried down as seedlings by a great avalanche on Dennison Mountain in December of 1867.

1 3/4 miles brings you to Ladybug Camp, elevation 4400 feet, where there are several flats along the river as well as pools for swimming and fishing. True to its name, this area is very popular with ladybugs. Across the river you see a waterfall on Garfield Creek.

As a historic footnote, the Ladybug Trail to this point is part of the historic Hockett Trail, built in 1862 as a route to connect Visalia, then the largest town in the southern San Joaquin Valley, with the silver mines in the Inyo and Coso Mountains east of the Owens Valley. This was during the Civil War, and the Owens Valley was full of transplanted southerners. There was some concern by the U.S government that the silver from those mines would go to the Confederates, so to protect the mines the Union sent troops to Fort Independence. The trail itself, however, was chartered by Tulare County, possibly to ensure that Fort Independence would be resupplied by the merchants of Visalia. The contract to build the trail was awarded to John B. Hockett. It began at Hale Tharp's ranch below Three Rivers, followed the South Fork to Hockett Meadow, descended to the little Kern, climbed Coyote Pass, crossed the Kern River at Lewis Camp, climbed Golden Trout Creek to Cottonwood Pass, then descended to the Owens Valley and Fort Independence.

From Ladybug Camp a non-maintained trail follows above the river for about another 1/4 mile before crossing the South Fork near a small grove of giant sequoias. That non-maintained trail continues all the way to Hockett Lakes but is very brushy in places.

From the west end of Ladybug Camp, the maintained trail continues from a wooden sign which reads, "Whiskey Log Camp 2.3 Miles" and climbs the south-facing slope. In the spring this grassy hillside is a beautiful flower show; on a winter day, it's the perfect place to bask in the sun.

The trail climbs through groves of black oaks and ponderosa pines. As late as the early 1970s, this trail was used by cattlemen driving their herds to Cahoon Meadow. Now all grazing leases within the boundaries of Sequoia National Park have expired.

At about 2 miles you have a fine view of Homer's Nose, the large granite dome to the north. As the story goes, in 1872 a government surveyor was in this area drawing up the original map; in his company was Joseph W. Homer, an early cattleman in Three Rivers. The surveyor looked up at the rock formation, then at Homer, and said, "Homer, that looks just like your nose." That name was recorded on the map, and it has remained so ever since.

For skilled mountaineers, it's possible to ascend the back side of Homer's Nose, by way of Cahoon Meadow.

To the east of Homer's Nose is a much smaller dome, Cahoon Rock, where there was once a fire lookout.

You now enter some very dense thickets of young cedars, as the trail traverses the mountainside. And at 3 miles you reach Cedar Creek, where there are good places to rest among a few medium-size sequoias.

Though the trail is not maintained beyond Cedar Creek, it's possible for experienced route finders to continue on to Whiskey Log Camp, 4 miles, elevation 5200 feet. The non-maintained trail ends at the South Fork of the Kaweah, 5 miles, elevation 6000 feet.

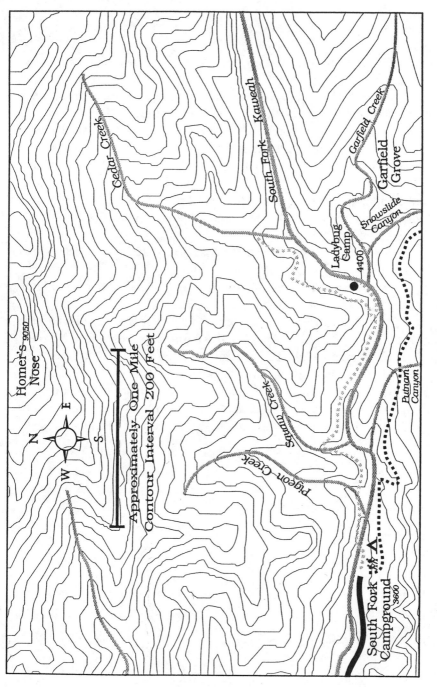

Garfield-Hockett Trail

GARFIELD-HOCKETT TRAIL

DISTANCE: 3 1/2 Miles (to Snowslide Camp)
HIKING TIME: 2 1/2 Hours (one way)
STARTING ELEVATION: 3600'
HIGHEST ELEVATION: 5850'
DIFFICULTY: Strenuous
USGS MAPS: Kaweah and Mineral King

Even though this is called the Garfield-Hockett Trail (because it passes through Garfield Grove and eventually leads you to Hockett Meadow), it should not be confused with the historic Hockett Trail. For a description of that trail, which follows the north side of the South Fork and is now known as the Ladybug Trail, see page 47.

The Garfield-Hockett Trail is steeper than most trails in the park but it's a well-maintained and beautiful trail, and those hikers with the stamina to give it a try will find it a rewarding experience.

Begin at South Fork campground. From Highway 198 in Three Rivers, follow South Fork Drive about 13 miles to the park entrance and campground. (See the map on page 10.) To find South Fork Drive on Highway 198, look for the fire station on the south side of the road about one mile east of Three Rivers Post Office.

There is no entrance fee or day-use fee at South Fork campground. Park at the day-use parking area at the entrance to the campground and look for the brown trailhead sign about 300 feet to the south. It reads, "Garfield-Hockett Trail."

As it leaves the campground the trail is very steep for the first 300 feet or so. It then levels off somewhat to merely steep and maintains this stubborn grade for most of the way. In its favor though, the trail has a canopy of black oaks shading its route for the first couple of miles.

By 1/2 mile you begin to have a view of Homer's Nose to the north. This massive landmark will be looking over your shoulder most of the hike.

You pass two unnamed creeks with cedars growing along their banks. Both of these creeks are often dry by midsummer.

1 1/4 miles brings you to Big Springs, elevation 4700 feet. While many of the creeks along this trail go dry in summer, Big Springs always maintains a fairly steady flow, even in years of extreme drought. Apparently its source is a large aquifer deep within the mountain.

At about 2 miles, and an elevation of 4950 feet, you come to Putnam Canyon. This is a snow avalanche chute, which is why there are no large trees growing in its drainage, only willow and thimbleberry.

Looking to the south, you can see the rocky cliffs of Dennison Mountain. On December 20, 1867, after days of snowfall followed by a warm rain, a section of Dennison Mountain 2 1/2 miles long collapsed in a huge avalanche that destroyed one third of Garfield Grove. When the dirt, rocks and debris settled at the bottom of South Fork Canyon, the flow of the river was blocked for several hours. When that dam finally gave way, a mountain of water roared down the canyon, devastating everything in its path. Giant sequoias were carried all the way to the valley floor, twenty miles away, and Visalia, more than forty miles away, was said to have been flooded with six feet of water.

The trail continues climbing steeply along the slope of Dennison Mountain. As late as the early 1980s, Dennison Mountain was one of the last refuges for wild California condors, a magnificent bird with a wingspan of nearly ten feet. In recent years, condors raised in captivity have been returned to the wild in southern California but with only moderate success.

At about 3 miles, and an elevation of 5600 feet, you come to the first sequoias in Garfield Grove, one of the largest sequoia groves in the park. It was named for President James Garfield, who was assassinated in 1881, just nine years before Sequoia became a national park.

The trail now becomes a bit less steep, at least for a ways.

As you hike through Garfield Grove, notice how few young sequoia seedlings there are. If you've hiked in Giant Forest and have seen the Park Service's prescribed burns there, you'll know that after a fire sequoia seedlings often sprout by the thousands. Sequoias are dependent upon fire to clear the organic material on the forest floor so the seeds can germinate in mineral soil, and to clear the canopy so young seedlings can receive sunlight. A lightning-caused fire burned part of Garfield Grove in July of 1986, but that fire does not appear to have produced very many seedlings.

At about 3 1/2 miles you come to Snowslide Canyon, elevation 5850 feet. Like Putnam Canyon, this is a snow avalanche chute. Snow from the avalanches pouring down all winter long often accumulates here in depths that are very unusual for such a low elevation. In a year of average snowfall, this part of Snowslide Canyon still contains snow as late as June. In a year of heavy snowfall, this canyon has been impassable to stock in mid-July.

Looking to the ridge to the east, you can see the tops of many giant sequoias which lie at the heart of Garfield Grove.

Less than 1/4 mile beyond Snowslide Canyon, there's a small flat below the trail with a fire ring and wooden stools. This is Snowslide Camp, a good turnaround point for a day hike. Just a few hundred feet beyond the camp is a small creek which runs year round.

If you choose to hike farther into Garfield Grove, 5 1/2 miles brings you to the Summit Trail, elevation 7300 feet, which follows Dennison Ridge. About 6 1/4 miles brings you to the eastern edge of Garfield Grove, elevation 7750 feet.

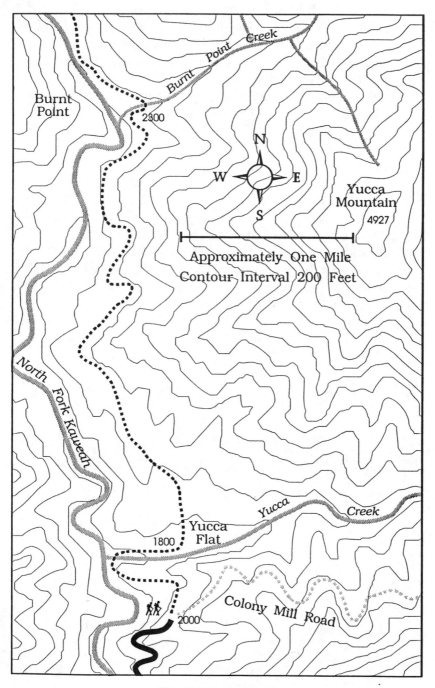

Burnt Point Creek

Burnt Point
2300

N
W · E
S

Yucca
Mountain
4927

Approximately One Mile
Contour Interval 200 Feet

North Fork Kaweah

Yucca Creek

Yucca Flat
1800

Colony Mill Road

2000

North Fork Trail

NORTH FORK TRAIL

DISTANCE: 4 MILES (to Burnt Point Creek)
HIKING TIME: 2 Hours (one way)
STARTING ELEVATION: 2000'
HIGHEST ELEVATION: 2400'
DIFFICULTY: Moderate
USGS MAP: Giant Forest

The original name for this trail was The West Boundary Truck Trail. It was built by the Civilian Conservation Corps in 1935, following the route of old wagon trails, and was used as a fire control road for this remote corner of the park. Now the road is closed to all vehicle traffic, and it is maintained as a trail.

From Highway 198 in Three Rivers, take North Fork Drive 10.2 miles to the end of the road. Though you are not yet inside the park boundary, it is permissible to use the small parking area here. Be sure not to block either of the gates, and be sure to lock your car. The dirt road leading uphill is the Colony Mill Road (see page 59). The road leading downhill takes you to Yucca Creek and the North Fork Trail.

Follow the road downhill for 1/2 mile, where you will come to a fence and white cattle guard which mark the park boundary. (The boundary at this point runs east and west, following the ridge top.) Continue down the road to a row of boulders which block vehicle access beyond that point. Walk around the boulders until you come to Yucca Creek, elevation 1600 feet. This is a year-round creek where there are good pools for swimming. If you leave the trail and follow the creek downstream, you soon come to the North Fork of the Kaweah, where there are also good swimming and fishing holes.

There was once a bridge over Yucca Creek, but it has washed out. Now all that remain are two large culverts which you must carefully pick your way across. On the north side of the creek the trail turns east, following above the creek.

At 3/4 miles you come to a fork in the trail. The fork to the right leads you on a detour to historic Yucca Flat and the old Grunigen Ranch.

If you choose to take this detour, another 1/4 mile brings you to a large grassy flat with two ponderosa pines and a sycamore. This general area was once the site of an Indian village, as potholes and pictographs a little farther up the creek demonstrate. Later, in the 1880s, it was homesteaded by members of the Kaweah Colony, a group of socialist utopians (see page 59). Years later it was known as the Burdick Ranch, and later yet it became the Grunigen Ranch. Eventually, the Park Service bought the 147 acres of the original homestead north of Yucca Creek, and in 1971 the old ranch house was torn down.

There is no trail following Yucca Creek, but it is possible to continue in that direction for about another 1/2 mile, after which the route becomes steep and very brushy.

Returning to the point where you began your detour, you now continue up the North Fork Trail. The trail climbs fairly steeply, passing over open, grassy hills that are very pretty in the spring and winter when they are green and covered with wildflowers.

After 1 3/4 miles, elevation 2400 feet, the trail levels off somewhat. Looking back to the south, you can see Ash Peaks, as well as part of the Colony Mill Road. To the west, the park boundary is the North Fork of the Kaweah. Beyond the river is land owned by the federal government (Bureau of Land Management) but leased to cattle ranchers.

Along the trailside you see a shrub with shiny, dark-green leaves. This plant, common throughout California, was named by Spanish priests. As the story goes, upon their early arrival to California the priests were plagued with chronic constipation caused by a diet of dried meat and hard biscuits. The Indians prescribed a tea made from this plant, and when the tea cured the fathers' constipation they named the plant "yerba santa," the holy herb.

At 2 miles you come to an unlocked gate. Here the trail makes a sweeping bend to the east, and you have a view of the upper North Fork. Looking due north, about 3 miles, you can see part of the original truck trail climbing the ridge to Hidden Springs.

2 1/2 miles brings you to an unnamed creek which flows from Yucca Mountain. You will notice that parts of Yucca Mountain are very badly overgrown with chamise, while other parts appear to be more open. The Park Service has been using prescribed burns here to reduce the age of the chamise stands, improve the animal habitat, and provide

a buffer zone for wildfires which might start outside the park. Because of the rugged nature of the area, the prescribed fires are lit by helicopters dropping a jellied gasoline mixture similar to napalm.

The trail continues to contour around Yucca Mountain to Burnt Point Creek, 4 miles, elevation 2300 feet. Here you see several steep, non-maintained footpaths leading down the creek to the river. You should only use these footpaths with extreme caution.

Burnt Point Creek makes a good turnaround point for a day hike, but the trail does continue more or less in the same fashion for about two more miles, where again there are non-maintained footpaths leading down to the river. The badly-eroded trail then becomes quite brushy after it begins climbing to Hidden Springs.

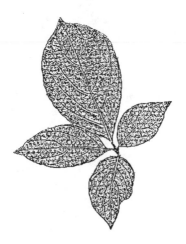

Dogwood

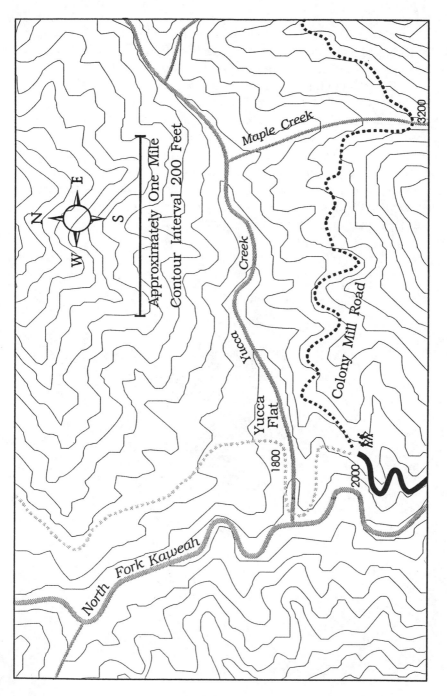

Colony Mill Road

COLONY MILL ROAD

North Fork to Maple Creek

DISTANCE: 2 3/4 Miles (one way)
HIKING TIME: 2 Hours (one way)
STARTING ELEVATION: 2000'
HIGHEST ELEVATION: 3200'
DIFFICULTY: Moderate
USGS MAP: Giant Forest

No trail in Sequoia National Park has a history more intriguing than the Colony Mill Road. In a sense, the very establishment of the park has its roots in this trail.

In 1885 a group of San Francisco-based socialist utopians, known as the Kaweah Colony, put together a plan for acquiring ownership of government timberlands in Giant Forest. This was before the establishment of Sequoia National Park, when only rough trails gave access to the remote plateau. The colonists' plan was for each individual in the group to file a federal claim for 160 acres. By pooling ownership of the lands, it would become economically feasible to build a road from Three Rivers to Giant Forest, where they would log and mill the lumber.

From 1886 to 1890, the colonists worked on their road, using almost nothing but hand tools. The quality of their work is evident in the remarkably even grade of the road and, particularly, in the rock walls which still remain in excellent condition. The colonists were able to complete their road as far as what is now called Colony Mill, at about the 5400-foot level. They set up a steam-powered mill and even processed some lumber.

Eventually, however, the colonists' plans were defeated when the federal government refused to grant them ownership of the lands they had filed on. In 1890 Giant Forest became part of the new Sequoia National Park, and not long after that the Kaweah Colony began to fall apart.

From Colony Mill, the road was extended to Giant Forest by the U.S. Cavalry in 1903, and that was the only route for vehicles into Giant Forest until 1926, when the modern route following the Generals Highway from Ash Mountain was completed.

Today the road is maintained as a trail from the end of North Fork Drive to the Crystal Cave Road. Though the day hike described here only goes as far as Maple Creek, it is possible to hike the entire length. (See page 109 for a description of the upper end of the Colony Mill Road.)

From Highway 198 in Three Rivers, take North Fork Drive 10.2 miles to the end of the road. Though you are not yet inside the park boundary, it is permissible to use the small parking area here. Be sure not to block either of the gates, and be sure to lock your car. The dirt road leading downhill goes to Yucca Creek and the North Fork Trail (see page 55). The dirt road leading uphill is the Colony Mill Road.

Take the uphill fork, going over or around the cable across the road. This is a public easement over private land, so stay on the road.

At 1/2 mile, near the top of the ridge, you reach a gate; if the gate is locked, go over, under or around it. A few feet farther, at the top of the ridge, elevation 2500 feet, is a park service gate marking the boundary of Sequoia National Park. This gate has a pedestrian bypass.

The trail now turns more easterly as it enters Yucca Creek Canyon. As you round the point of the ridge, you are looking down on Yucca Flat. (See page 55 for a description of that historic site.) Looking to the east you see pine-covered Colony Peak.

At 1 mile you come to a drainage with a year-round spring. If you look about fifty-feet up the drainage, you can see an old concrete water tank that was once used for filling fire trucks.

As you can see, the Colony Mill Road was too narrow for two lanes; the uphill and downhill traffic had to go in shifts. Park visitors waited at the Kaweah post office for a park ranger to lead them in convoy to Giant Forest.

By 1 1/4 miles you can see more to the northeast, and now have a view of Little Baldy.

There are some very dense thickets of poison oak on both sides of the road. In the winter, after the leaves have fallen, some people may not recognize this troublesome plant. Look for the small, pale berries and the vine-like shoots. Remember that even the oil residue on the bark can cause a rash.

This road is traveled heavily by bears. Look for their tracks in the soft dirt or mud, and for their mounds of scat.

You pass several unnamed creeks, as the trail meanders up the side of Ash Peaks Ridge.

Anyone who has ever worked the dumb end of a pick and shovel will appreciate the labor the Kaweah Colonists put into their road along this section. Considering the rugged terrain it traverses and the era in which it was built, the quality of this road is remarkable.

At 2 3/4 miles, elevation 3200 feet, you come to Maple Creek, where there are indeed maple trees as well as a few alders. This makes a good destination for a day hike, but if you're feeling ambitious you can continue as far as Colony Mill Ranger Station, about 8 miles, elevation 5400 feet, and to the Crystal Cave Road, about 10 1/2 miles, elevation 5300 feet.

Black Oak

Live Oak

INTRODUCTION to GIANT FOREST

One of the first things you'll notice about Giant Forest, after you're able to take your eyes off the immense sequoias, is that the terrain here isn't nearly as steep and rugged as other areas of the park. The temperature is neither as hot as the foothills nor as cold as some of the higher alpine areas. Poison oak is absent, rattlesnakes are rare, and the scenery is unlike any other place on earth. In short, Giant Forest comes very close to being a day hiker's paradise.

After a glance at a map of the area, you'll see that Giant Forest is a bewildering maze of hiking trails. In fact there are nearly fifty miles of maintained trails crisscrossing the Giant Forest plateau. An imaginative hiker could invent any number of loops or one-way hikes beginning and ending almost anywhere. Remember, however, that even those hikers familiar with Giant Forest can sometimes become disoriented. The Giant Forest area is heavily wooded and flat enough that distant landmarks aren't always easy to see. A map is mandatory; use either the maps in this guidebook, the USGS topographic maps, or buy the excellent park service map of Giant Forest that sells for about $1.50 at the visitor centers.

In the next few years you'll be seeing some important changes taking place in Giant Forest. The Park Service is in the process of removing nearly all buildings from Giant Forest. It has become obvious in recent decades that these structures are not compatible with the long-term health of the sequoia groves. Most of the buildings are very old and are in need of replacement. Rather than begin rebuilding a small city in the middle of one of the world's finest stands of giant sequoias, the Park Service has decided to move all tourist facilities to Clover Creek, about five miles to the north, on the Generals Highway. Most of the support systems (roads, power, water and sewer) are already in place at Clover Creek. By the end of the 1990s, the move should be complete.

In recent years the Park Service has added a summer shuttlebus system to the Giant Forest-Lodgepole area. It runs between the Lodgepole Visitor Center, Sherman Tree, Giant Forest, Moro Rock and Crescent Meadow. This can be a great benefit to day hikers trying to get back to their trailhead without retracing their steps.

Throughout the Giant Forest area you will see the evidence of many recent fires. Almost all of these were set intentionally by the Park Service as part of their prescribed burn policy. The purpose of the policy is to remove the heavy accumulation of fuels on the forest floor, to thin the dense vegetation, and to encourage the establishment of sequoia seedlings and other species which rely on fire. Some people will find the burned areas of Giant Forest stark and unsettling. But as you come to understand the natural role of fire in this ecosystem, the burned areas become interesting and even beautiful. In the southern Sierra Nevada, fire has always been a natural element of the ecosystem, and we must learn to live with it if we are going to pass these parks on to future generations of humans, plants and animals.

One last note: While hiking in the Giant Forest area you'll see yellow metal triangles nailed to trees about ten feet above the ground. These markers designate winter ski trails. Though some of the ski trails correspond roughly to the hiking trails, the yellow markers should not be relied upon as guides. Follow the trail signs and the descriptions in this guidebook.

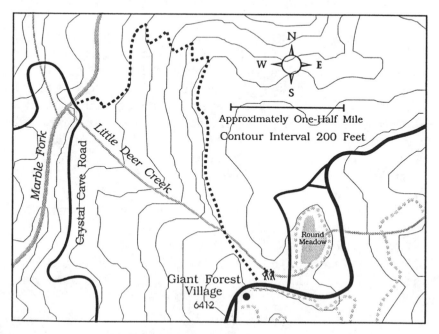

Marble Fork Bridge Trail

MARBLE FORK BRIDGE TRAIL

DISTANCE: 3 1/2 MILES (one way)
HIKING TIME: 1 1/2 Hours (one way)
STARTING ELEVATION: 6400'
LOWEST ELEVATION: 5100' (Marble Fork Bridge)
DIFFICULTY: Moderate

This is a lazy hiker's trail—almost all downhill. It's also a very scenic trail and is used less often than most trails in Giant Forest. The only drawback is that after you've completed the hike you must walk back uphill to the trailhead or arrange for a ride to meet you at the Marble Fork Bridge.

The trailhead can be found at the east end of the parking area for Giant Forest Village. At the stop sign, look north across the Generals Highway to a trail sign which reads, "Sunset Rock 0.8—Marble Fork Bridge 3.4."

In just a few hundred feet, you cross a wooden foot bridge over Little Deer Creek and come to a trail junction. Take the upper trail, the paved trail, toward Sunset Rock.

At 1/4 mile you come to a small meadow known as Eli's Paradise. Notice the peculiar sequoia growing there; it once lost its crown, perhaps by lightning, and a large limb has turned skyward to become the new crown.

As you round the point of the ridge, you have a view of Little Baldy to the north.

3/4 miles brings you to Sunset Rock, a large granite dome which provides a fine view of the Marble Fork of the Kaweah, as well as a view of the Ash Peaks Ridge and Colony Mill to the west.

The trail now begins a long descent through white firs, sugar pines, cedars, and thousands of dogwoods. With their steel gray bark, bright green leaves and white blossoms, dogwoods are one of the most beautiful trees in the Sierra, and this trail has the best display of dogwoods of any trail in the park. Even after the flower petals drop, the red fruit clusters give color to the trees. In the fall, when their leaves turn brilliant red, dogwoods are at their finest. It's said that dogwoods got their name because it was once believed that a concoction made from the bark was useful in treating dog mange.

The trail follows a series of switchbacks down the north-facing slope. At 2 miles you come to a break in the forest; here you can look down into the Marble Fork canyon and hear the river's rushing current. Looking up the Marble Fork (east), you can see nearly as far as Lodgepole.

At 2 1/2 miles, and an elevation of about 6000 feet, you begin to see a few black oaks, with their large leaves and dark bark. Of all the acorns available for food in central California, the Indians favored acorns from black oaks over all others because of their large size and because they are said to be sweeter than other acorns. You can judge their flavor for yourself, but keep in mind that the Indians had to use boiling water to leach the bitter and toxic tannic acid from all acorns.

3 1/2 miles brings you to the Marble Fork Bridge, where you will hopefully have a vehicle waiting for you.

To reach the Marble Fork Bridge by vehicle from Giant Forest, drive west on the Generals Highway 2.1 miles to the Crystal Cave Road; turn right (north), and drive 1.7 miles to the Marble Fork Bridge. There's a parking area .2 miles beyond the bridge. (Note: Between Labor Day and Memorial Day the Crystal Cave Road is closed just past the Marble Fork Bridge. After the first heavy snowfall of the winter, the Crystal Cave Road is closed at the Generals Highway until the road is cleared again in the spring. To find out how far the road is open at any particular time, call the park at (209) 565-3341.)

For fishermen, it's possible to walk from the Marble Fork Bridge upstream for 1/4 mile following the south side of the river, and to walk downstream for 1/4 mile following the north side of the river. There is no maintained trail in either direction, and the granite banks are steep and slippery. This area is not suitable for children or novice hikers. Use extreme caution, especially in the spring and early summer when the water level is high.

General Sherman Tree

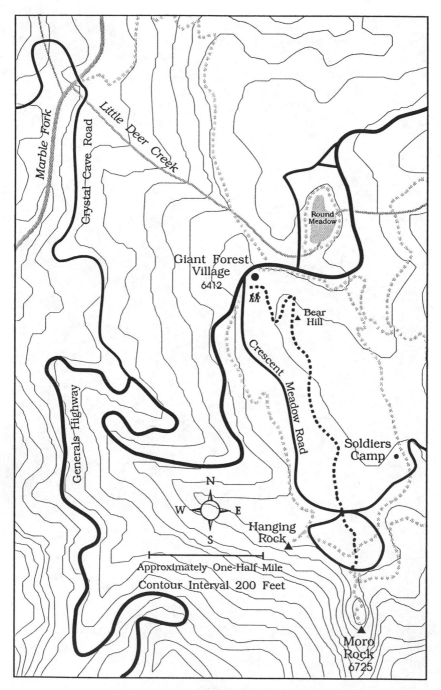

Bear Hill Trail

BEAR HILL TRAIL

DISTANCE: 2 Miles (one way)
HIKING TIME: 1 1/2 Hours (one way)
STARTING ELEVATION: 6400'
HIGHEST ELEVATION: 6600'
DIFFICULTY: Moderate
USGS MAP: Giant Forest

In the early days of Giant Forest, Bear Hill was a trash dump. It was named Bear Hill because of the large number of black bears that gathered there to root through the fresh garbage. During the 1920s and '30s, one of the major tourist attractions at Giant Forest was to gather every evening on Bear Hill to watch park rangers supervise the feeding of the black bears. At one time there were even bleachers set up for viewing this spectacle.

Nowadays, of course, we know that feeding the bears does them a great disservice by conditioning them to become dependent upon man for food. Rather than supervise the feeding of the bears, park rangers today are doing everything they can to persuade visitors not to feed the bears.

Leave your car at the parking area in front of Giant Forest Village and follow the Crescent Meadow Road about 1/4 mile from the Giant Forest store. On the left side of the road (east) you see a trail sign that reads, "Bear Hill .5 Miles."

As you start up the hill, you can see that this was once a road, later replaced by the Generals Highway, and now maintained as a trail.

The trail climbs moderately through white firs, sugar pines, sequoias and dogwoods. 1/2 mile brings you near the top of Bear Hill, elevation 6600 feet. At the trail junction, take the right-hand fork, which cuts back sharply to the southwest. From here on the trail is mostly downhill.

At 3/4 miles you see an interesting pair of sequoias. At one time they grew so closely together they nearly touched, but fire has now hollowed out a chamber between them.

Notice the heavy layer of dead trees and limbs, known as forest litter, that has accumulated here in the last one hundred years. This is a result of man's suppression of fire, which in the natural ecosystem of the Sierra Nevada turns out to be a very bad idea.

In another 1/4 mile you come to an area that has been intentionally burned by the Park Service. Most of the trees killed by the fire are young white firs. Though the sequoias have taken a few burn scars, they are mostly unaffected by the fire due to their thick, fire-resistant bark.

As you can see, one burn kills so many firs it only increases the forest litter; a second fire is then necessary to clean up the trees killed by the first fire. Eventually, the forest floor will be open and clear, giving species other than white firs a chance to compete.

At 1 1/2 miles, looking west, you see the Auto Log on Crescent Meadow Road.

You climb a short hill, then drop down to the Crescent Meadow Road. To stay on the Bear Hill Trail, follow the right (south) fork of the road, staying to the right when the road forks again. You then see a trail sign marking where the Bear Hill Trail begins once more.

Another short climb brings you to the Roosevelt Tree, one of far too many sequoias in this park named after dead politicians and military men. This odd practice of naming an ancient tree after a man of status and privilege began in the early days of the Park Service when it was necessary for environmentalists to appeal to the vanity of politicians. It's said that John Muir himself named this tree after Theodore Roosevelt in 1902.

At the trail junction, follow the fork to the right (west). Then you drop quickly to the Moro Rock parking area, elevation 6400 feet.

For a hiking route that will return you to Giant Forest Village, see the Soldiers Trail, on page 97, or catch the shuttlebus.

Castle Rocks

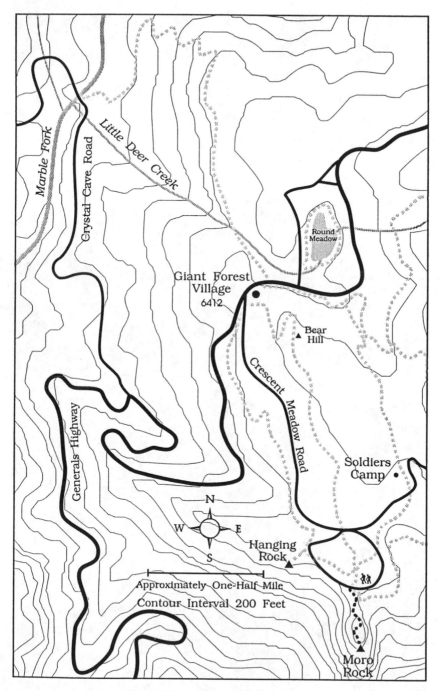

Marble Fork

Crystal Cave Road

Little Deer Creek

Round Meadow

Giant Forest Village
6412

Bear Hill

Crescent Meadow Road

Generals Highway

Soldiers Camp

N

W   E

S

Hanging Rock

Approximately One-Half Mile
Contour Interval 200 Feet

Moro Rock

Moro Rock Climb

MORO ROCK CLIMB

DISTANCE: 1/4 Mile
HIKING TIME: 1/2 Hour
STARTING ELEVATION: 6400'
HIGHEST ELEVATION: 6725'
DIFFICULTY: Easy
USGS MAPS: Giant Forest

This short climb is really more like a stairway than a trail. But it's fun, and anybody in reasonably good condition, even children, can finish it. No visit to Giant Forest would be complete without a quick jaunt to the top of Moro Rock.

The Moro Rock parking area is on the Crescent Meadow Road, 1.5 miles from Giant Forest Village. Before climbing the rock, stop to read the interpretive sign explaining its formation.

Remember, there have been people killed and injured by lightning on Moro Rock. Do not climb the rock if there are dark clouds nearby, thunder, hail, rain, or if you can hear or feel static electricity in the air.

The granite stairs are steep, windy, and can be slippery. Keep children under control at all times.

From the top of Moro Rock you have an excellent view of the Great Western Divide to the east. A permanent map is placed here to help you identify the distant peaks.

Many visitors to the park don't realize that what they're seeing is not the main crest of the Sierra Nevada, but the Kaweah Range, which was termed the "Great Western Divide" by geologist Joseph Le Conte in 1896. Several peaks along this divide are close to 14,000 feet high and rival the main crest in their grandeur. Mount Whitney, on the main Sierra crest but blocked from view, is almost due east from here.

The panorama you see from Moro Rock represents only about one fifth of Sequoia National Park. Together with Kings Canyon, the two parks total 864,383 acres. Of that, 736,980 acres are wilderness. The Sequoia-Kings Canyon Wilderness, together with the Golden Trout Wilderness, the John Muir Wilderness, the Ansel Adams Wilderness, the Yosemite Wilderness, and several smaller wilderness areas, make up one of the largest contiguous blocks of wilderness in the lower forty-eight states, extending 150 miles down the backbone of the Sierra Nevada.

To the south and west you can see the Middle Fork of the Kaweah, as well as the town of Three Rivers. On a clear day you can even see the Coast Range, 110 miles to the west. Unfortunately, clear summer days are rare. Smog drifting in from the urban areas of California is probably the single greatest threat to Sequoia National Park. Recent studies have shown that one third of the trees in the park show some damage by smog. Until man learns to restrain his use of fossil fuels, even remote wilderness areas are not truly protected.

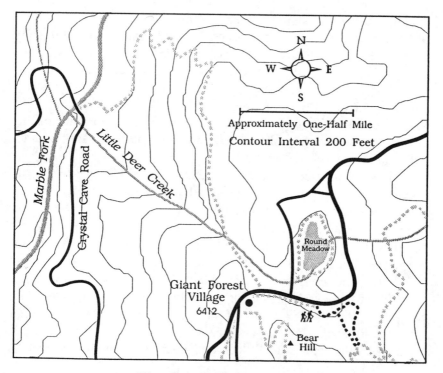

Hazelwood Nature Trail

HAZELWOOD NATURE TRAIL

DISTANCE: 1 Mile (a loop trail)
HIKING TIME: 1 Hour
STARTING ELEVATION: 6400'
HIGHEST ELEVATION: 6500'
DIFFICULTY: Easy
USGS MAP: Giant Forest

The Hazelwood Nature Trail is a self-guided nature trail, and a very easy trail—perfect for the first day out or for hiking with small children.

The trail begins on the Generals Highway, .3 miles east of Giant Forest Village. Look for the sign that reads, "Hazelwood Nature Trail Parking Area." You will find additional parking just across the Generals Highway.

In the early days of Sequoia National Park, the Hazelwood area was one of seven extremely popular campgrounds in and around Giant Forest. There was no limit on how long campers could stay, and some campers made Hazelwood a kind of second home, adding walls, roofs and fences to their nearly permanent campsites. During the Great Depression, homeless people would "camp" here for months at a time, and eventually these campgrounds took on the appearance of shanty-towns.

Even in those early days, the Park Service was aware that the sequoias of Giant Forest were not reproducing, and as more research on giant sequoias became available, it became apparent to the Park Service that the shallow root systems of the sequoias were being seriously damaged by the compaction caused by roads and other human trampling. If the sequoias were to be preserved for future generations to enjoy, campgrounds like Hazelwood would have to go.

Between 1936 and 1939, the Park Service built the large camp-grounds at Lodgepole and Dorst (both of them out of the sequoia groves), and began closing Hazelwood and other campgrounds in Giant Forest. This huge task of relocating tourist facilities out of Giant Forest is still in process, but is expected to be complete some time in the late 1990s.

Because there are interpretive signs along its route, the Hazelwood Nature Trail won't be described in further detail here. The trail signs are color coded; follow the signs with purple lettering.

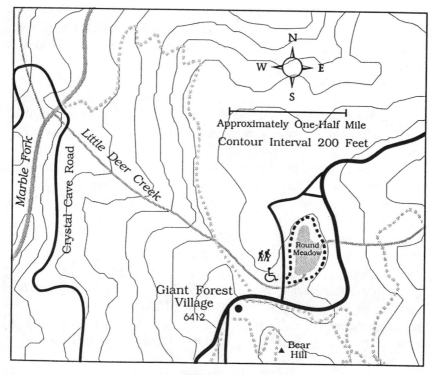

Round Meadow Loop

ROUND MEADOW LOOP

Trail For All People

DISTANCE: 1/2 Mile (a loop trail)
HIKING TIME: 1/2 Hour
STARTING ELEVATION: 6400'
HIGHEST ELEVATION: 6400'
DIFFICULTY: Easy
USGS MAP: Giant Forest

The Round Meadow Loop is a paved, self-guided nature trail with wheelchair access and a very gentle grade. It was built mostly with private donations, and was completed in September of 1989.

The trailhead for the Round Meadow Loop is at the Round Meadow parking area. On the Generals Highway, 0.2 miles east of Giant Forest, look for the sign that reads, "Round Meadow—Trail For All People." Turn north and drive 0.1 miles to the parking area.

During the early years of the Sequoia National Park, Round Meadow was the center of activity for Giant Forest. Before the automobile, tourists who arrived at the park by horse and wagon grazed their stock in the meadow, often leaving nothing but bare stubble by midsummer. Later, restaurants, stores and other tourist accommodations were built around the fringes of the meadow. When park superintendent John White arrived here in 1920, he described the scene: "... it was barely possible to see Round Meadow because of the tents which surrounded it ... and in every direction there were pit toilets, cess pits, and a criss-cross of water lines under the Big Trees."

When the Generals Highway was built in 1926, the park's concessions were moved to the area now known as Giant Forest Village. As you can see, Round Meadow has greatly recovered from its earlier traumas.

Because there are interpretive signs along the route of this trail, it won't be described in further detail here.

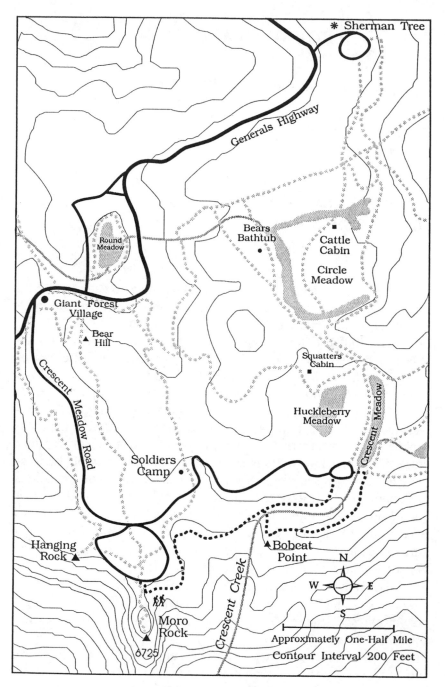

Sugar Pine Trail

SUGAR PINE TRAIL

DISTANCE: 1 1/2 Miles (one way)
HIKING TIME: 1 Hour (one way)
STARTING ELEVATION: 6400'
HIGHEST ELEVATION: 6700'
DIFFICULTY: Moderate
USGS MAPS: Giant Forest and Triple Divide

This airy trail offers an opportunity to see the devastating effects of a wildfire, plus the site of an ancient Indian village. There's also a lofty overlook from which it's possible to see the original trail to Giant Forest. In the fall and early spring, this trail is pleasantly sunny due to the southern exposure, but if you're planning on hiking it in the summer, try for a morning start.

The Sugar Pine Trail begins at the Moro Rock parking area, on the Crescent Meadow Road, 1.5 miles from Giant Forest Village. Look for the sign marking the trailhead at the southeast end of the parking area.

The trail immediately drops a hundred feet, then begins contouring the south-facing slope. It's easy to see that this trail got its name from the many fine examples of sugar pines along its route. Sugar pines are a five-needle pine with short needles and reddish-brown bark. The largest sugar pines often grow to eighty inches in diameter. They also have very long, crooked branches, which give mature sugar pines a distinctive asymmetrical shape. The largest pine cones you see lying around Giant Forest are from the sugar pine.

Sugar pines are being threatened by blister rust, a fungus that was originally found only in Europe. It was accidentally introduced to this continent by a professional botanist who brought an infected specimen of white pine back with him from Europe. Host plants in the life cycle of blister rust are the Ribes, commonly known as gooseberries and currants. During the 1940s and '50s, the government tried to stop the spread of blister rust by attempting to eradicate all the Ribes in the Sierra Nevada. Not surprisingly, that effort was unsuccessful, and blister rust continues to spread. In recent years however, there has been some success in identifying those sugar pines which show a natural resistance to blister rust. By selecting seeds from these trees, the U.S. Forest Service and Park Service hope to develop a new generation of sugar pines.

As you continue along the trail, you soon begin to see the disastrous effects of the Buckeye Fire, which was started in October of 1988 by a carelessly discarded cigarette on the Middle Fork, 3000 feet below. The fire quickly roared up the chaparral-covered slope to the Crescent Meadow Road. Much of the credit for stopping the fire at that point is given to the park's prescribed burn policy, which over the years had been reducing fuel north of the road. Still, this area along the Sugar Pine Trail was at the fire's head and took the most scorching heat. The devastation is obvious. Sadly, the fire cost the Park Service $2.5 million to extinguish—enough money to fund a prescribed burn policy for all of Sequoia-Kings Canyon for the next ten years.

You now pass a small creek with ferns growing in its bed, and at 1 mile you come to a trail sign which reads, "Crescent Meadow .5 Miles."

At 1 1/4 miles you come to a fork in the trail. Both trails will take you to Crescent Meadow, but the trail on your right (south) is probably the more interesting of the two.

As you cross Crescent Creek, you see several Indian mortar holes, used for grinding seeds and acorns. This area was a summer village site for the Indians who wintered along the lower Kaweah River. Like almost all Indian village sites in the Sierra, this one is situated in a place with good exposure to the southern sky, which promised warm sunny days in the spring and fall.

You now climb a short, steep hill until you reach Bobcat Point, where there's a fine view of the Middle Fork of the Kaweah. The striking rock formations directly across the canyon are known as Castle Rocks.

If you look below you, and slightly up canyon, you can see the route of the original trail into Giant Forest. From the Middle Fork it meandered up the steep slope and into Crescent Meadow.

On the skyline to the southeast you can see Sawtooth Peak, which overlooks Mineral King Valley.

You now climb another short hill before arriving at the Crescent Meadow parking area, elevation 6700 feet. If you don't have a ride waiting, you can catch the shuttlebus back to your car. Check the schedule posted on the bulletin board in front of the restroom.

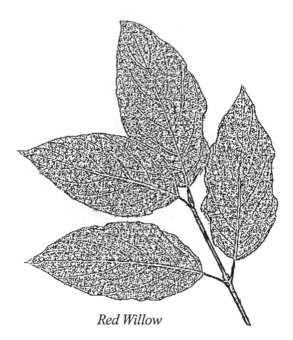

Red Willow

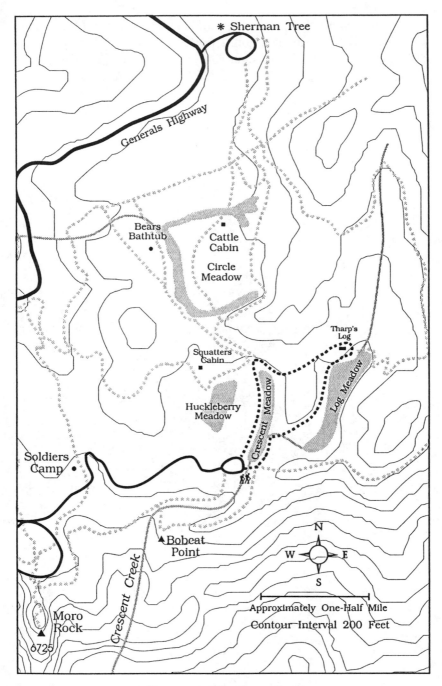

Crescent Meadow Trail

CRESCENT MEADOW TRAIL

DISTANCE: 1 3/4 Miles (a loop trail)
HIKING TIME: 1 1/2 Hours
STARTING ELEVATION: 6700'
HIGHEST ELEVATION: 6850'
DIFFICULTY: Easy
USGS MAP: Triple Divide

This is probably the most popular short hike in Giant Forest, and with good reason. The hiking is easy, the scenery as fine as any in Giant Forest, and the history intriguing. It's also one of the best short hikes for young children.

The trail signs along the Crescent Meadow Trail are color coded; follow the signs with orange lettering.

Beginning at the southeast end of the Crescent Meadow parking area, hike south across the two wooden bridges over Crescent Creek. If you're hiking with young children, be sure to have them say hello to the trolls who live under these bridges.

By leaving the trail here and hiking up the creek just two hundred feet, you can see a few Indian bedrock mortars. This was a summer village site of the Indians who wintered along the lower Kaweah River. At the time when white explorers and settlers first came to Tulare County, the Indians inhabiting most of the foothills were Monaches, related culturally and linguistically to the Owens Valley Paiutes. Farther back in time, however, much of the foothills, and possibly this village site, were occupied by Yokuts.

You now round the southern end of Crescent Meadow and soon see Log Meadow to the east. Cattle grazing hasn't been allowed in most of Sequoia National Park for more than one hundred years. Compare the thick, lush grasses and sedges in Log Meadow with other meadows you may have seen outside the park where cattle grazing is allowed.

At 1 mile you come to Tharp's Log, a true "log" cabin and the oldest structure of any kind in the park. Beginning with a fire-hollowed sequoia, the builder of this unique dwelling added a rock chimney, then closed off one end of the log with redwood shingles.

Hale Tharp, a prospector and later a cattleman, is usually credited with being the first white man to see Giant Forest, in the summer of 1858. We have no way of knowing whether he was the first white man here or not. Early American settlers reported that there were Mexican soldiers, who had deserted the missions along the coast, living with Indians in the Sierra foothills. It's possible these deserters saw Giant Forest before Hale Tharp.

At any rate, Hale Tharp was an unusual white settler in that he liked and respected the Indians at a time when nearly all white settlers in California were feuding with them. Tharp built his permanent home on Horse Creek (below the present town of Three Rivers), just a short distance from a Yokuts village, and befriended the Indians by bringing them deer and other game. "They were honest and kind to each other," he wrote. "I never knew of a murder or theft amongst them."

The Indians also liked and respected Tharp. They told him stories of a place up in the mountains with lush meadows and trees larger than any he could imagine. To satisfy his curiosity, Tharp asked the Indians to take him there, which they did: "I made my first trip into Giant Forest in the summer of 1858," he wrote. "We went in by way of the Middle Fork and Moro Rock and camped a few days at Log Meadow. I do not remember the dates that we were there, but I carved with my knife on a redwood log my name and the date. These figures and my name should still show. I had two objects for making this trip; one was for the purpose of locating a high summer range for my stock, and the other was due to the fact that stories the Indians had told me of big trees caused me to wonder, so I decided to go and see."

Tharp eventually homesteaded the Log Meadow area, and spent several summers running his cattle here. It isn't known for certain though whether or not he actually built the cabin which bears his name. (At any rate, it was later rebuilt.) We do know that the great wilderness gadabout, John Muir, begged a little bread from Tharp and spent a few nights at this camp in the summer of 1875. Apparently Muir, who bragged of heading into the mountains with nothing but a great coat, a pocketknife and a single loaf of bread, relied on others who went into the mountains better prepared.

At the north end of Tharp's log is a trail junction. The trail to the right (east) leads you around Log Meadow and back to Crescent Meadow. To stay on the Crescent Meadow Trail, take the trail to your left (west).

At 1 1/4 miles you come to the Chimney Tree, a standing, dead sequoia hollowed out by fire. This was a living tree until 1919, when it was killed by a fire started by a careless camper. Here you see a confusing trail sign which indicates that the Crescent Meadow parking area can be reached in both directions. Take the trail to your right (west).

A short distance brings you to another junction. Take the trail to your left (south), and follow the edge of Crescent Meadow back to the parking area.

Thimbleberry

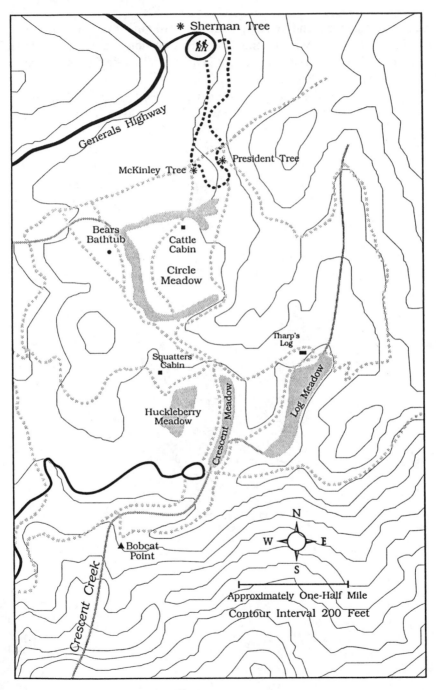

Congress Trail

CONGRESS TRAIL

DISTANCE: 2 Miles (a loop trail)
HIKING TIME: 1 1/2 Hours
STARTING ELEVATION: 6800′
HIGHEST ELEVATION: 7000′
DIFFICULTY: Easy
USGS MAPS Giant Forest and Triple Divide

The Congress Trail is a self-guided nature trail giving access to some of the largest sequoias in the park. It's also one of the most heavily-used trails in the park and therefore not for those hikers looking for seclusion. The trail bed is paved the entire way and is very easy to follow. For a small donation, a pamphlet is provided by the Park Service at the trailhead. Because there are interpretive signs the entire way, the trail won't be described here except to say that it begins at the General Sherman Tree parking area. Look for the trailhead at the northeast end of the parking area. The trail signs are color coded; follow the signs with yellow lettering.

And while you're at the Sherman Tree parking area, go have a look at the world's largest living thing. There are trees with greater diameters, and many of the coastal redwoods are taller, but considering its entire mass, the General Sherman tree is the world champion. One little-known fact is that it was originally named the Karl Marx Tree by the Kaweah Colonists, a group of utopian socialists who built the first road to Giant Forest. (See page 59 for more information on the Kaweah Colonists.)

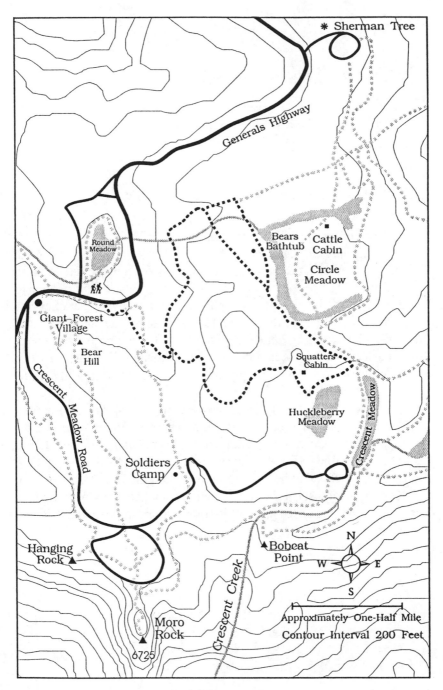

Huckleberry Trail

HUCKLEBERRY TRAIL

DISTANCE: 4 Miles (a loop trail)
HIKING TIME: 3 Hours
STARTING ELEVATION: 6400'
HIGHEST ELEVATION: 6900'
DIFFICULTY: Moderate
USGS MAPS: Giant Forest and Triple Divide

The Huckleberry Trail is one of the most rewarding medium-distance trails in Giant Forest. It isn't used as much as the Congress Trail and Crescent Meadow Trail, yet it offers several interesting sights, including a century-old cabin and an ancient Indian village site.

The beginning of the Huckleberry Trail can be bit confusing. Follow the map provided here and remember that the trail signs along the Huckleberry Trail are color coded; follow the trail signs with blue lettering.

Begin at the Hazelwood Nature Trail parking area, on the Generals Highway, .3 miles east of Giant Forest Village.

Hike the first half mile of the Hazelwood Nature Trail, a self-guided nature trail with interpretive signs along its route. At each junction you come to, head south, until you see the big sign with blue lettering which marks the start of the Huckleberry Trail.

You round a small creek and meadow growing thick with ferns. Then, at 1/2 mile, you come to a trail junction that reads, "Huckleberry Meadow 1 Mile." Head west, climbing the steep hill through the sequoias, white firs and dogwoods.

1 1/2 miles brings you to the Squatter's Cabin, a log structure dating to the 1880s. It's called the Squatter's Cabin because it was built without right or title on land that had been previously homesteaded. Inside the cabin, notice the rock fireplace with a lintel made from a four-foot slab of granite. An interpretive sign tells more about the cabin.

Hiking east from the Squatter's Cabin, you soon come to a trail junction. Looking to the east, you see a corner of Crescent Meadow. Now take the trail to your left (north), up the short steep hill.

At the next trail junction you begin to see Circle Meadow. Veer to the left (northwest).

After following the edges of Circle Meadow for 1/4 mile, you come to a trail junction. To the right (northeast) is Bear's Bathtub. This short detour off the Huckleberry Trail brings you to a pair of sequoias grown together with a fire scar between them; this hollow is filled with dank, dark water. The unlikely story is told that Chester Wright, an old-time mountain guide, once surprised a bear wallowing in this water, hence the name Bear's Bathtub.

Continue on the Huckleberry Trail to the left (northwest), and 3 miles brings you to the Washington Tree, elevation 6800 feet. This is one of the largest sequoias in the park, almost as big as the Sherman Tree. One branch of the Washington Tree, about halfway up, is larger than most of the surrounding fir trees.

While you are near the Washington Tree, notice the thousands of young sequoia seedlings which have germinated here since the last prescribed burn, in the late 1970s. Sequoias do not reproduce very well without fire to open the cones and to clear a seed bed on the forest floor. Not all of these seedlings will survive, of course, but enough will survive to guarantee the regeneration of this particular grove.

Also, notice how many of the white firs here have not survived the last fire. Many people don't like to see dead trees, but in this situation they're a positive sign. White firs grow very rapidly, can tolerate shade, and therefore crowd out many of the other tree species, including sequoias. To establish a healthy forest of mixed conifers, fire is needed to thin out some of the white firs.

Continue along the Huckleberry Trail until you reach the Alta Trail. Turn left (west), and continue to Little Deer Creek.

On both sides of Little Deer Creek you can see Indian mortar holes where Indians ground seeds and acorns. Some of the largest holes are three feet in diameter, and their purpose is considered something of a mystery. The most likely theories are that they were used as baking pits, or as vats for tanning hides.

By late summer, running water is often scarce in much of Giant Forest, but Little Deer Creek is always reliable, even in a severe drought. This, no doubt, is why the Indians chose this site for their summer village. Notice how dark the surrounding soil is after centuries of campfires.

At the next trail junction, the trail to your right (north) returns you to the Generals Highway, 1/4 mile away. Continuing on the Huckleberry Trail, you contour around the north-facing slope.

3 1/2 miles brings you to the end of your loop. Follow the western half of the Hazelwood Nature Trail back to the parking area.

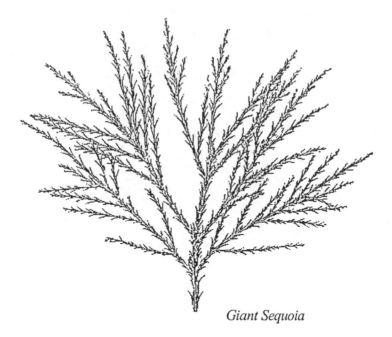

Giant Sequoia

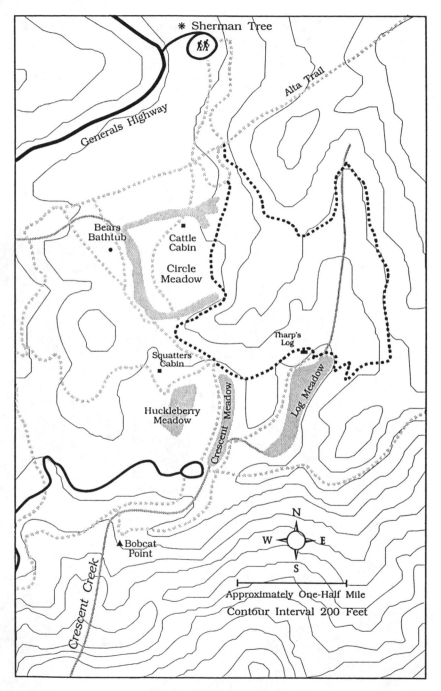

Trail of the Sequoias

TRAIL OF THE SEQUOIAS

DISTANCE: 6 Miles (a loop trail)
HIKING TIME: 4 Hours
STARTING ELEVATION: 6800'
HIGHEST ELEVATION: 7300'
DIFFICULTY: Moderate
USGS MAPS: Giant Forest and Triple Divide

The Trail of the Sequoias gives access to some of the plateau's more remote areas and is perfect for hikers and picnickers looking for a longer hike into the heart of Giant Forest. Though the difficulty is only moderate, the distance may be a bit far for young children. If you wish to shorten this hike, it's possible to end at Crescent Meadow and have a vehicle meet you there, or better yet, ride the shuttlebus back to the Sherman Tree. The trail signs are color coded; follow the signs with green lettering.

The Trail of the Sequoias begins at the General Sherman Tree parking area. Look for the trailhead at the northeast end of the parking area.

For the first 3/4 miles, you follow the same easy route as the Congress Trail. At the junction of the Alta Trail, however, you leave the Congress Trail and proceed south, uphill. Look for the sign with green lettering which reads, "Trail of the Sequoias."

The next half mile or so is the steepest part of this hike, so go slowly and enjoy the many fine specimens of giant sequoias.

At 1 1/2 miles you reach the ridge forming the backbone of Giant Forest, the highest point on this hike. Looking across the canyon to the east, see if you can pick out the rounded shapes of the large sequoias growing on the hillside. Views such as this can be seen nowhere else in the world except the southern Sierra Nevada, and they define the character of Sequoia National Park.

You now descend to Crescent Creek, then begin contouring through the sequoia groves you saw earlier from the ridge. Notice the broad range in character of the sequoias here: some are postcard perfect, while some have had their tops blasted out by lightning; some have had their tops die back, only to begin again with a former branch serving as the new crown; others have been dead for hundreds of years, yet stubbornly refuse to fall over.

Of those sequoias that have fallen, notice how shallow their root systems are. In fact the largest trees in the world have root systems much more shallow than the smaller firs and pines nearby. Sequoias lack a tap root, which on a typical ponderosa pine grows many feet into the ground. For this reason, sequoias only thrive in areas where strong winds are rare. Even so, toppling by wind is the most common cause of death for large sequoias.

At 3 miles you begin to see green patches of Log Meadow through the trees to the west. You come to several minor trail junctions in the next mile, but in each case take the trail to your right.

You descend quickly to Log Meadow now and skirt its upper end until you reach Tharp's Log, described on page 83.

Pick up the trail again on the northeast end of Tharp's Log and follow it around the log until you begin heading west. You follow part of the Crescent Meadow Trail now for a short ways.

You pass the Chimney Tree, a huge dead sequoia hollowed out by fire, and at about 4 miles you leave the Crescent Meadow Trail. Follow the green-colored sign to your right (north).

(If you wish to shorten your hike at this point, you can follow the orange-colored signs to Crescent Meadow and, perhaps, catch the shuttlebus back to the Sherman Tree. Check to see if the bus is running before you begin this hike.)

In another hundred feet you join a short section of the Huckleberry Trail. At this junction, turn north and follow the green and blue sign which reads, "Sherman Tree."

The trail climbs steeply now for a short ways. Near the top of the ridge, you leave the Huckleberry Trail and follow the sign to Circle Meadow.

After hiking only a few hundred feet farther, you can see Circle Meadow. At the trail junction you have two options. Both options are roughly the same distance and difficulty, and both return you to the Sherman Tree parking area:

Option 1: Stay on the Trail of the Sequoias, following the fork to the right (northeast). You skirt the edge of Circle Meadow, then proceed to the Senate Group, distance 5 miles, where you will rejoin the Congress Trail. Turn to your left (west), and follow the paved trail back to the Sherman Tree parking area.

Option 2: This is the more interesting of the two options. Take the fork to your left (northwest). The trail immediately crosses a narrow band of Circle Meadow and continues to the Black Arch, a large sequoia gutted by fire so that just a rim of live wood survives. You are now on a small plateau surrounded by Circle Meadow, a fine place to stop and enjoy the solitude.

At 4 1/2 miles you come to a junction. Proceed to your right (northeast) to the Cattle Cabin, a good place to wait out an afternoon thunder shower. The Cattle Cabin was built by ranchers who grazed their stock in the Giant Forest area. An interpretive sign there tells more about the cabin.

You now cross another stringer of Circle Meadow, cross the Alta Trail, and at the McKinley Tree rejoin the Congress Trail, distance 5 miles. Follow the paved trail north to the Sherman Tree parking area.

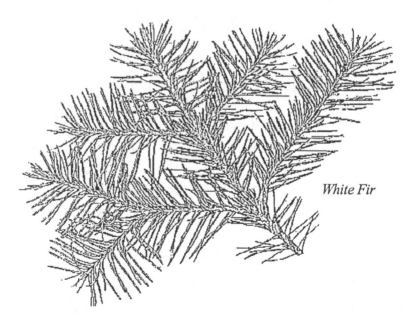

White Fir

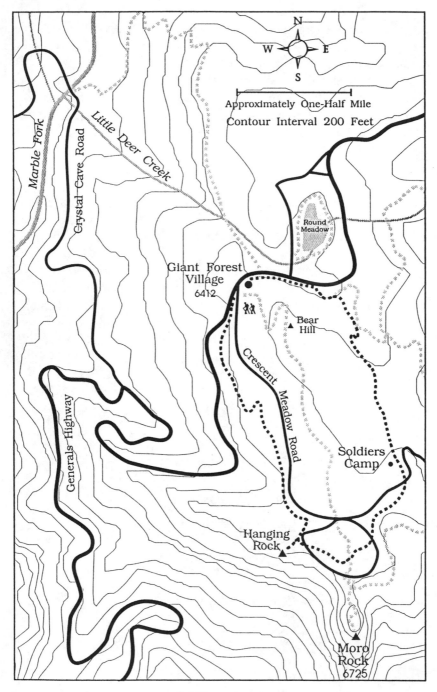

Soldiers Trail

SOLDIERS TRAIL

DISTANCE: 4 1/2 Miles (a loop trail)
HIKING TIME: 3 Hours
STARTING ELEVATION: 6400'
HIGHEST ELEVATION: 6800'
DIFFICULTY: Moderate
USGS MAP: Giant Forest

Although the Soldiers Trail is a loop trail, the first half (from Giant Forest Village to Moro Rock) parallels the Crescent Meadow Road most of the way and therefore can't be considered an ideal hiking experience. The entire loop is described here, but you may want to hike only the second half of the trail (Moro Rock to Giant Forest Village). One suggestion would be to hike the Bear Hill Trail from Giant Forest Village to Moro Rock, then hike the Soldiers Trail back to Giant Forest Village. Or, ride the shuttle bus from Giant Forest Village to Moro Rock, then return to the Village by way of the Soldiers Trail.

The trail signs for the Soldiers Trail are color coded; follow the signs with red lettering. (Note: Some signs may refer to this trail as the Moro Rock Trail, or the Moro Rock—Soldiers Trail. For the purposes of this guidebook, it's simply the Soldiers Trail.)

Begin at Giant Forest Village at the junction of the Generals Highway and the Crescent Meadow Road. Walk west on the Crescent Meadow Road for one hundred feet until you see the sign marking the trailhead on the right side of the road. It reads, "Moro Rock Trail."

The trail contours gently around the west end of the Giant Forest plateau, offering occasional views of the San Joaquin Valley to the west. At 1/2 mile you pass near a small stringer meadow and see several sequoias that have been blown over. Sequoias have very shallow roots and can't tolerate strong winds. Here on the edge of the plateau, with no protection to the west, they are sometimes exposed to powerful wind storms.

1 1/4 miles brings you to a short detour to Hanging Rock. From Hanging Rock you have a good view of the lower Middle Fork of the

Kaweah, as well as the Ash Peaks Ridge. If you look carefully, you can see the location of the Colony Mill Ranger Station, almost due west. Near that saddle is where the Kaweah Colonists assembled their sawmill in the summer of 1890. The first road into Giant Forest came over that saddle, by way of the North Fork of the Kaweah, and then up what is now the Crystal Cave Road. The modern highway you see below you, to Giant Forest by way of Ash Mountain and Deer Ridge, wasn't built until 1926.

From the Hanging Rock junction, cross the Crescent Meadow Road and pick up the trail again about 200 feet south.

At 1 3/4 miles you come to a junction directly above the Moro Rock parking area. If you're en route to Moro Rock, continue to the south. If you're continuing on the Soldiers Trail, cut back sharply to the northeast.

If you're starting the Soldiers Trail at Moro Rock parking area, look for the trailhead at the extreme eastern end of the parking area. Walk uphill (north) to the junction described in the paragraph above.

A short, steep climb brings you to the Roosevelt Tree, named for Teddy Roosevelt, supposedly by John Muir. Continuing in an easterly direction, at 2 miles you cross the Crescent Meadow Road and pass by the Triple Tree, an unusual configuration of sequoias.

At 2 1/2 miles you again cross the Crescent Meadow Road, within sight of Tunnel Log.

On your right (east) you see a very lush meadow. On the knoll just to the west of the meadow was the site of Soldiers Camp. From 1891 until 1913, Sequoia National Park was guarded by the U. S. Cavalry. Their job was to protect the giant sequoias from loggers, and to protect the wildlife from poachers. They also worked on the road from Colony Mill to Giant Forest, which was completed in 1903 and first allowed motor vehicles to reach the park. The soldiers chose this site for their camp because of the nearby water and grazing for their horses; most of the other meadows in Giant Forest were already taken by cattlemen. If you look around Soldiers Camp, you see old rock fire rings and rock-lined pits which were part of the original camp. Imagine the thoughts of the young soldiers camped here among the giant sequoias, and the letters they must have sent home describing trees which many people in the world refused to believe even existed.

Continuing north, as you pass through an area of prescribed burns initiated by the Park Service, notice how many young sequoia seedlings have sprouted here. Fires help to open the sequoia cones so the tiny seeds can be released, and the fires clear the forest floor so the seeds can reach the soil to germinate. Also, fires open the forest canopy so the young seedlings can receive sunlight. In fact it's rare to see sequoia seedlings in areas where there haven't been recent fires.

You now climb over the ridge which divides Giant Forest. You pass by the Broken Arrow, an oddly-shaped burnt sequoia, then quickly drop down the other side of the ridge.

At 3 1/2 miles you come to several trail junctions. Continue straight ahead, downhill, until you reach the Hazelwood Nature Trail. Follow the west half of that trail nearly to the Generals Highway, where you see a sign with red lettering which reads, "Village." Follow that paved trail west to Giant Forest Village.

Bracken Fern

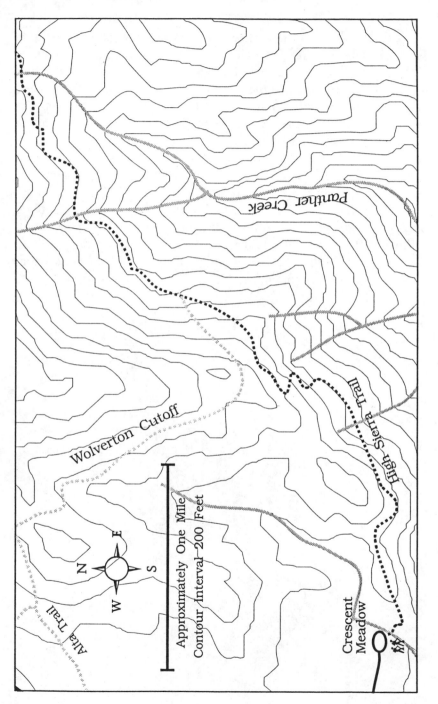

High Sierra Trail

HIGH SIERRA TRAIL

DISTANCE: 4 1/2 Miles (one way to Panther Creek)
HIKING TIME: 3 Hours (one way)
STARTING ELEVATION: 6700'
HIGHEST ELEVATION: 7200'
DIFFICULTY: Moderate
USGS MAP: Triple Divide

The High Sierra Trail is one of the most famous, and most popular, backpacking trails in the park. It was built during the years from 1927 to 1932, and was designed to be a fast and relatively easy route into the backcountry of the Kern River Canyon, which Sequoia National Park didn't acquire until 1926. Bearpaw, Kaweah Gap, Kern River and the summit of Mount Whitney are but a few of the destinations along its route.

Besides the vast backcountry portion of the High Sierra Trail so popular with backpackers, its first few miles are also excellent for day hikers. Its steady, moderate grade allows hikers to cover a lot of miles with a minimum of effort, and it provides spectacular views of the Middle Fork of the Kaweah and of the Great Western Divide. Also, because of its south-facing exposure, the High Sierra Trail is pleasantly warm in the late fall and early spring. In the summer, the trail can be hot, so plan an early start if you're hiking during that season.

The High Sierra Trail begins at the Crescent Meadow parking area. Starting at the restroom, take the paved trail south. Cross the two wooden bridges over Crescent Creek, and you soon come to a trail junction. Tharp's Log is to the left, the High Sierra Trail is to the right, uphill.

You climb the north-facing slope, passing through an area that was burned by the Park Service in the early '80s. This was once a tangled mass of downed trees and young saplings. The controlled burns have been very successful in creating a more healthy forest here.

By 1/2 mile you cross over a ridge to the south-facing slope. Here you see the disastrous effects of the Buckeye Fire of 1988, which was started by a carelessly discarded cigarette on the Middle Fork of the Kaweah, 3000 feet below.

At 3/4 miles you come to Eagle View, where you have the first of many good views of the Kaweah Range, or Great Western Divide. The Kaweah Range was termed the Great Western Divide in 1896 by the geologist Joseph Le Conte; his intention, apparently, was to keep it from being confused with the main crest of the Sierra Nevada, which is due east but hidden from view. The rocky crags to the south are known as Castle Rocks.

The trail is almost level now until you come to a few gentle switchbacks. It then levels off again for at least a mile. At about 2 1/4 miles you round the point of a ridge and come upon a good view of Panther Rock, to the north. Looking more to the east, you can see Alta Peak and Alta Meadow.

2 3/4 miles brings you to the Wolverton Cutoff. Look for two old wooden signs nailed to a small tree below the trail. The Wolverton Cutoff itself can be seen on the uphill side, along with a metal sign. That trail is primarily a stock route between Wolverton Corrals and the High Sierra Trail, but it's also possible to use the Wolverton Cutoff as a route to the Sherman Tree (see page 105).

Another few hundred feet brings you to a fork of Panther Creek, with a small waterfall above the trail. Even in the driest of years, this small creek runs cool and clear and makes a good resting place.

At 3 1/4 miles you reach another fork of Panther Creek. Directly above you are the pink and gray crags of Panther Rock.

After crossing a couple more small creeks, you reach the final fork of Panther Creek, in a fairly deep and eroded ravine.

Giant Forest in Winter

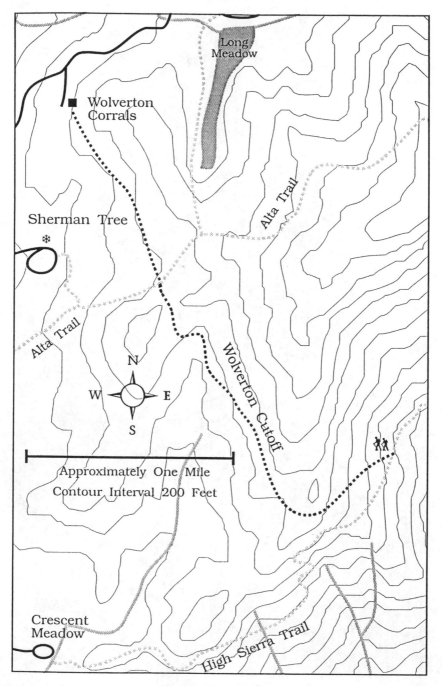

Wolverton Cutoff

WOLVERTON CUTOFF

DISTANCE: 7 Miles (one way)
HIKING TIME: 4 Hours (one way)
STARTING ELEVATION: 6700′
HIGHEST ELEVATION: 7600′
DIFFICULTY: Strenuous
USGS MAP: Triple Divide

The Wolverton Cutoff passes through a beautiful corner of Giant Forest that is seldom seen by most park visitors. The trail is used primarily as a stock route between Wolverton Corrals and the High Sierra Trail, but by using the shuttlebus, or arranging for a ride to meet you at the end, it can be made into a very fine day hike.

If it weren't for the long distance (7 miles) this trail would only be rated as moderate. Except for one short mile, the entire way is gently graded.

As you can see by the accompanying map, there are several ways to begin and end this hike, but perhaps the easiest is to begin at Crescent Meadow and end at the Sherman Tree.

From the Crescent Meadow parking area, follow the High Sierra Trail for the first 2 3/4 miles. (For a complete description of the High Sierra Trail, see page 101.)

At 2 3/4 miles you reach the Wolverton Cutoff. Look for two old wooden signs nailed to a tree below the trail, and a metal sign above the trail. Here you cut back sharply to the west and start uphill.

The Wolverton Cutoff begins climbing moderately steep switch-backs up the south-facing slope. The next mile is the most work you will do on the entire trail. You pass through a thick forest of white fir, as well as an area badly burned in the Buckeye Fire of 1988.

At about 3 3/4 miles, and an elevation of 7600 feet, you reach the ridge top, which is the highest point on this trail as well as one of the highest points in Giant Forest. Here you have an exceptional view of the Great Western Divide and a good place for a rest.

Almost immediately after starting down the north side of the ridge, you begin seeing giant sequoias, as well as several small meadows. This area gives you an idea of what Giant Forest must have looked like before the first white settlers arrived. The next two miles are excellent for spotting wildlife, particularly bears, so be quiet and watch carefully.

The trail now drops only slightly as it contours around the ridge side.

In addition to some very beautiful and symmetrical sequoia specimens, you pass several gnarled and misshapen sequoias—some of the strangest trees to be found anywhere. Also, you pass a large sequoia which has fallen in the relatively recent past, perhaps during the high winds of June 1971.

At 4 3/4 miles you cross Crescent Creek, round the point of a knoll, and begin dropping until you reach a small meadow thick with ferns and lupine. Here you strike the Alta Trail, 5 3/4 miles, elevation 7300 feet. You turn west (left) on the Alta Trail and descend quickly through a very pretty grove of sequoias.

At 6 1/4 miles you come to the paved Congress Trail. Here you turn north and follow the trail signs to the Sherman Tree parking area, 7 miles.

If you don't have a ride waiting for you, it might be possible to catch the shuttlebus back to Crescent Meadow. Or, if the shuttlebus isn't running, you can return to Crescent Meadow without retracing your steps by way of the Trail of the Sequoias. See page 93 for a description of that trail.

Puffballs

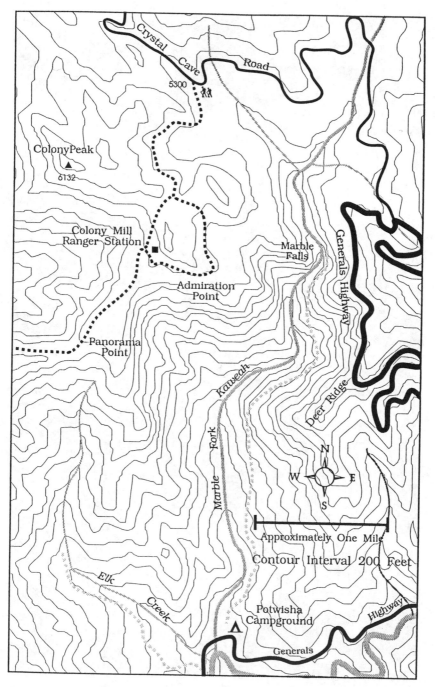

Colony Mill Road

COLONY MILL ROAD

Crystal Cave Road to Colony Mill Ranger Station

DISTANCE: 2 1/2 Miles (one way)
HIKING TIME: 1 1/2 Hours (one way)
STARTING ELEVATION: 5300'
HIGHEST ELEVATION: 5700'
DIFFICULTY: Moderate
MAP: Giant Forest

The Colony Mill Road has more history haunting its crooked miles than any other trail in the park. To truly understand the vision and stamina of the Kaweah Colonists who built this road in the 1880s, you have to walk its route.

To plan this hike properly, you should call the park service, at (209) 565-3341, and ask if the Crystal Cave Road is open. Generally, the Crystal Cave Road is locked at the Generals Highway after the first heavy snowfall of the year and not reopened until spring. Also, after Labor Day the Crystal Cave Road is locked just west of the Marble Fork Bridge. Even if the Crystal Cave Road is locked, however, it is permissible for you to hike along it.

To find the trailhead for the Colony Mill Road, take the Generals Highway to the Crystal Cave Road, about 2 miles below (west) of Giant Forest Village. Follow the Crystal Cave Road 1.7 miles to the Marble Fork Bridge, elevation 5100 feet. If the road is closed, use the parking area 0.2 miles beyond the bridge.

If you are either hiking or driving on the Crystal Cave Road, begin looking for the trailhead for the Colony Mill Road approximately 2 1/2 miles west of the Marble Fork Bridge, on the left (west)) side of the road. There is no sign marking the trailhead, but look for several large logs placed there to block vehicle access. The elevation at the trailhead is 5300 feet.

The Colony Mill Road, now maintained as a trail, starts downhill for the first few hundred feet, then begins climbing moderately and maintains that grade for at least the next mile. Because it was once a road, the trail is exceptionally wide and the grade remarkably even. Here and there, on the downhill side, you can see some fine examples of century-old rock riprap supporting the trail bed. For a brief history of the Colony Mill Road, and the Kaweah Colonists, see page 59.

The trail passes through a dense forest of mixed conifers and dogwoods, allowing few distant views.

Keep in mind that you are seeing the park as visitors saw it a hundred years ago. Before the construction of the modern road to Giant Forest, in 1926, the Colony Mill Road was the only route for motor vehicles into the park, and the entrance station was at Colony Mill. In 1903 only 450 park visitors found their way up this road to Giant Forest. By 1913 that figure had climbed modestly to 3,823 visitors. With the completion of the modern road in 1926, park visitation rose dramatically and by 1939 the number was 275,329 visitors. Today Sequoia receives more than 1 million visitors each year.

At 1 1/2 miles, near the top of a ridge (elevation 5700 feet), you come to a fork where a faint, non-maintained and fairly brushy trail takes off to the right (west, uphill). That trail offers an alternate return route, so note its location but stay on the main trail heading left (south, downhill).

The trail descends moderately, and at 2 miles you reach Admiration Point, where you have an eagle's view of the Marble Fork of the Kaweah, some 2000 feet below.

The trail now turns in a more westerly direction, and at 2 1/2 miles you come to the Colony Mill Ranger Station, elevation 5400 feet. Near this site the ill-fated Kaweah Colony set up their steam-powered lumber mill, fondly nicknamed Ajax, which milled very little lumber—certainly not enough to justify building a road by hand all the way from Three Rivers.

In later years, after the establishment of the park in 1890, this was the site of a ranger station, which is abandoned and dilapidated now, but still standing. Always a lonely outpost during most of the year, it's even more lonely now, and haunted by the ghosts of frustrated rangers still waiting for their transfer to Yosemite Valley.

Less than 1/4 mile beyond the ranger station, the road forks. The uphill trail leads you in a loop 1/2 mile back to the fork described above at 5700 feet. Though this alternate return route is not maintained, and is brushy in places, it's easy enough to follow. The other fork continues down the Colony Mill Road.

If you choose to continue down the Colony Mill Road, the trail follows a route along Ash Peaks Ridge. This part of the road is rarely visited anymore, but it makes a very pleasant fall or spring hike. Also, because of the steep cliffs and deep canyons, it makes a particularly good place to spot raptors.

At 3 1/2 miles you come to a saddle overlooking Elk Creek (see page 27). At one time a trail descended from this point all the way to the Middle Fork of the Kaweah. Another trail from this point climbed to a fire lookout tower on Ash Peak. Both trails are overgrown with brush now, though you can still see their faint traces in some places.

If you wish, you can follow the Colony Mill Road all the way to North Fork Drive, elevation 2000 feet, distance about 8 miles. See page 59 for a description of that end of the trail.

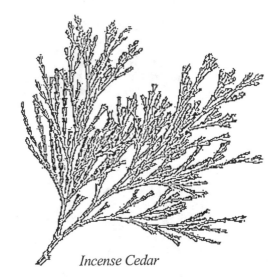

Incense Cedar

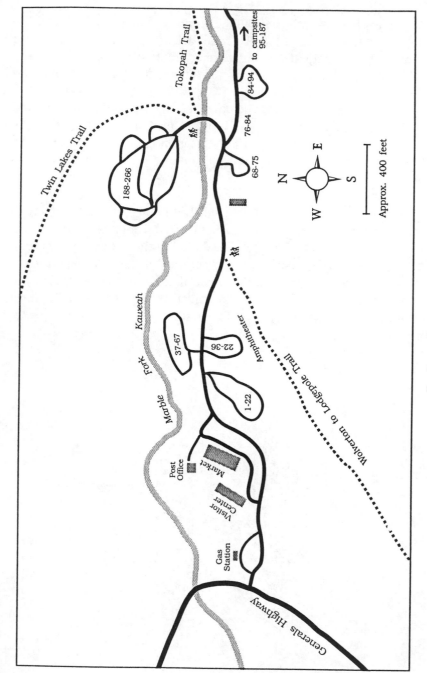

Lodgepole

Introduction to Lodgepole

and

Wolverton

Although they are only a few miles apart, the Lodgepole and Giant Forest areas are so different from one another they could be in entirely separate parks. While Giant Forest is a relatively flat and heavily-wooded plateau, much of Lodgepole is steep, rocky and rugged. While Giant Forest has deep organic soils, Lodgepole has been scoured by glaciers which left only thin mineral soils. And there are no giant sequoias in Lodgepole—not one.

The Indians also recognized an important difference between Giant Forest and Lodgepole. At Lodgepole you will find almost no evidence of Indian habitation, while Giant Forest, on the other hand, has several village sites. If you've ever spent a night at Lodgepole campground, you will understand the most likely reason why this is so. At night, as the cold air on the peaks to the east of Lodgepole settles, that cold air is funneled into Tokopah Valley. Sometimes even in the summer Lodgepole can be very cold at night. Giant Forest, on the other hand, with its warm southern exposure and its dense forests, tends to gain and retain heat. Even in the late fall, temperatures in Giant Forest can be moderate.

Many of the trails out of Lodgepole and Wolverton lead to areas with elevations above 9000 feet. Most hikers will feel the effects of the altitude: shortness of breath, lack of energy, and perhaps headaches. You must remember to go slowly here, and to give your body time to adjust.

If you're a frequent visitor to Lodgepole, you will have noticed several changes and additions here in the last decade. There's a new ranger station and visitor center, and a new market complete with deli, ice cream shop, laundromat and showers. Just a mile away, at Red Fir, there's a new maintenance facility, and at Clover Creek you'll find the beginnings of an entirely new resort area.

The Park Service's plan is to remove almost all structures from the Giant Forest area and relocate them in the Lodgepole and Clover Creek area. Most of the old buildings were decaying anyway, and the infrastructure, such as the sewer and power lines, needed major work. Rather than rebuild what amounted to a small city in the heart of one of the finest sequoia groves in the world, the Park Service made the wise decision to move all new facilities to the less fragile Clover Creek area. The move should be complete by the end of the 1990s.

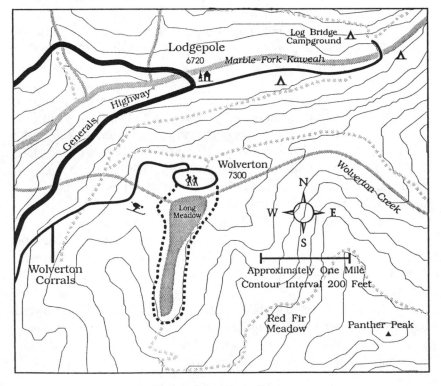

Long Meadow Loop

LONG MEADOW LOOP

DISTANCE: 2 Miles
HIKING TIME: 1 Hour
STARTING ELEVATION: 7300'
HIGHEST ELEVATION: 7400'
DIFFICULTY: Easy
USGS MAP: Triple Divide

This easy trail is just long enough to stretch your legs. It's perfect for young children, offers views of an open meadow, plus gives you a look at an Indian village site. If this is your first day at Lodgepole, this trail would be a good choice.

During the summer, the first half of this trail is used as a horse trail by the Wolverton Pack Station. If you should meet horses on this trail, please remember that the proper trail etiquette is for hikers to step off the trail on the downhill side and stand quietly until the horses have passed.

There is no trail sign marking this trail, so you must watch carefully for its start. At the southeast end of the Wolverton parking area, near the restroom and looking south across Wolverton Creek, you see a small rocky knoll just 200 feet from the pavement. A faint path leaves the parking area, crosses Wolverton Creek on a pair of culverts, then climbs the rocky knoll.

At the top of the rocky knoll you can see a few shallow Indian mortar holes in the rocks. A summer village site was located here. Every summer the Monache Indians, who had permanent village sites in the foothills, migrated to the higher elevations where the hunting was better and the summer heat much more tolerable.

Now head uphill in a southeasterly direction, following only a faint trail for about 500 feet, until you strike the well-worn horse trail. You continue now in a southerly direction until you approach the edge of Long Meadow.

For many years this was an alpine ski area, complete with T-Bar and rope tow, but it received such little use that the facilities were removed in the early Nineties. Wolverton is still popular, however, with cross-country skiers.

During the early part of this century, Long Meadow, and in fact most of the Wolverton area, came very close to being flooded by a reservoir that was to store water for a hydroelectric plant. At that time this was private land, owned by the Mount Whitney Power Company, the same company that built the flumes on the Middle, East, and Marble Forks of the Kaweah, as well as the low dams on the lakes above Mineral King Valley. The company clearcut about one hundred acres in preparation for the dam, which was to be one hundred feet tall. But their plans failed when the engineers were unable to find a bedrock foundation in the glacial debris. Later, Southern California Edison Company, which acquired Mount Whitney Power Company's assets, donated this land to the Park Service.

After following the edge of the meadow, you climb a couple of short switchbacks before crossing the small creek which drains Long Meadow, then round the tip of the meadow and begin the homeward leg.

At 1 Mile you come to a trail junction and a wooden sign which points uphill and reads, "Alta Trail." Here you leave the worn horse trail and take the downhill trail north (right).

You descend again to Long Meadow and follow the meadow's edge through lodgepole pines, quaking aspens, red firs and ponderosa pines.

Resist the temptation to cut across the meadow. Continue 1/4 mile until you see a footpath turning east and following a culvert over Wolverton Creek. This returns you to the Wolverton parking area.

On Alta Peak

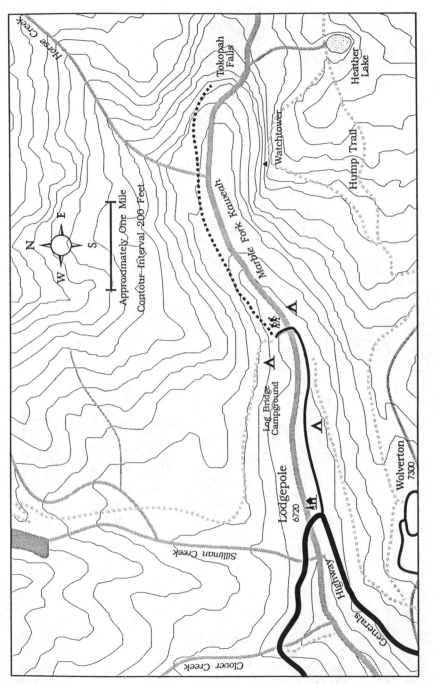

Tokopah Falls Trail

TOKOPAH FALLS TRAIL

DISTANCE: 1 3/4 MILES (One way)
HIKING TIME: 1 Hour (one way)
STARTING ELEVATION: 6800'
HIGHEST ELEVATION: 7300'
DIFFICULTY: Moderate
USGS MAP: Triple Divide

The name Tokopah is a Yokuts Indian word meaning "high mountain valley." But the Yokuts didn't give that name to Tokopah Valley—it was named by Walter Fry, superintendent of Sequoia National Park from 1912 to 1920. Furthermore, at 6800 feet the valley really isn't all that high. Yet, like Yosemite, Tehipite, Kings Canyon and other glaciated valleys on the western slope of the Sierra Nevada, Tokopah has the appearance of being much higher than it actually is. Also like those other famous valleys, Tokopah is a place of unusual beauty.

The trailhead can be found at the east end of Lodgepole, near the Log Bridge over the Marble Fork of the Kaweah. (The bridge now has steel girders but retains its original name.) Park on the south side of the river, in the parking area downstream from the bridge. A sign marking the trailhead is just north of the bridge.

The trail follows the Marble Fork of the Kaweah, maintaining a moderate grade the entire way. Like other valleys on the western slope of the Sierra, Tokopah was scoured by glaciers about 10,000 years ago. Along the valley floor where the river has swept away the soil, you can see the polished granite which is characteristic of glacial valleys. In some places on the sheer cliffs you can see horizontal lines gouged into the granite by boulders being dragged along the edge of the glacier.

The trees here are a healthy mixture of red and white firs, lodgepole pines, ponderosa pines and cedars. Along the river you can see willows, aspens and bitter cherry.

At about 1/2 mile you reach a clearing which allows a view of the upper valley. The impressive rock formation on the south wall is the

Watchtower. From the Pear Lake Trail you can reach the summit of the Watchtower and view Tokopah Valley from an entirely different perspective.

As you cross the fragile meadows, please stay on the rock causeways built there to protect the meadow vegetation from trampling. Before the causeways were built, there were several muddy footpaths leading through these meadows.

Along the middle portion of the trail you can find many quiet places along the river for fishing, swimming, or just resting in the shade. Remember though, particularly when the water level is high, that the river can be dangerous. Keep young children away from the water's edge.

At 1 1/4 miles you cross Horse Creek on a wooden bridge. As you can see by the channel which this steep creek has cut for itself, there are times when it carries a considerable volume of water. Even though the Horse Creek drainage is only a couple of miles long, it's almost all bare granite, with very little soil to absorb the moisture, and with any rainfall the entire runoff immediately rushes to the bottom.

At 1 1/2 miles you emerge from the forest and come within sight of the falls. The trail now climbs through huge granite boulders that have tumbled down from the cliffs above. Take note of the fine trail work through this talus slope: a route was blasted through the boulders, then a bed of riprap was tediously laid; finally a layer of hand-crushed rock was added to the surface. Like many trails in the park, this trail was built by the Civilian Conservation Corps.

The many talus caves among the boulders here are favored by marmots, fat coarse-haired animals about the size of a spoiled house cat. They are sometimes known by the less-flattering name, "whistle pig." Successful male marmots become polygamists, taking several females as their mates. Their habit of basking in the sun all day may seem like laziness, but it's actually a very practical strategy for storing body fat by expending the least amount of energy possible.

In the spring of a wet year, the mist from Tokopah Falls can drench you from a quarter-mile away. But by autumn of most years, its torrent has become barely a trickle. Notice the brown mineral stain on the rocks all around the falls caused by centuries of evaporating mist.

If you look on the cliff walls to the north and east of the falls, you will see a few juniper trees growing from the cracks in the rock.

There is no trail or footpath beyond the falls. There have been several injuries and fatalities of hikers trying to climb beyond this point. Unless you're an experienced rock climber with the proper equipment, do not venture beyond the falls.

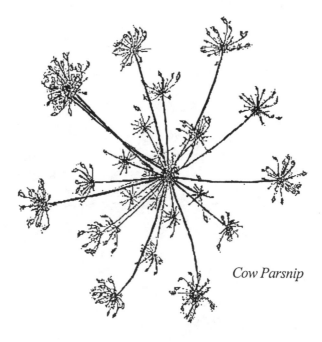

Cow Parsnip

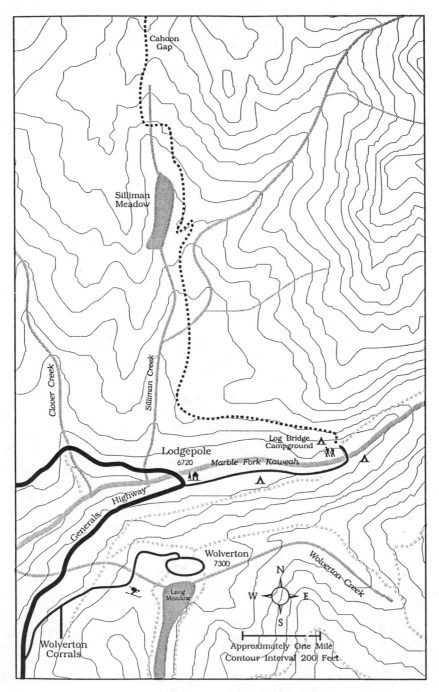

Twin Lakes Trail

TWIN LAKES TRAIL

DISTANCE: 2 Miles to Cahoon Meadow, 5 miles to Clover Creek

HIKING TIME: 2 Hours to Cahoon Meadow, 4 Hours to Clover Creek

STARTING ELEVATION: 6800′

HIGHEST ELEVATION: 8650′ (Cahoon Gap)

DIFFICULTY: Moderate to Cahoon Meadow, Strenuous to Clover Creek

USGS MAP: Triple Divide

Even though this is called the Twin Lakes Trail, all but the hardiest hikers will find it difficult to reach Twin Lakes and return in one day. Still, there are many fine destinations along this trail, and the route is interesting and varied. If you have already hiked the Pear Lake Trail and found that route to be more crowded than you would like, you'll find the Twin Lakes Trail to be a less-traveled alternative. Most hikers will find Cahoon Meadow to be a reasonable destination for a day hike.

The trailhead can be found at the east end of Lodgepole, near the Log Bridge over the Marble Fork of the Kaweah. (The bridge now has steel girders but retains its original name.) Park on the south side of the river, in the parking area west (downstream) of the bridge. Walk along the road, cross the bridge, and continue past the Tokopah trailhead. The Twin Lakes Trail begins about 200 feet north of the bridge.

The trail skirts the edge of Log Bridge campground, then begins a moderately steep climb up the south-facing side of the valley. In the summer this portion of the trail can be warm, so try for an early start.

The low-growing shrub with the sticky leaves and pungent smell is known as bear clover, or sometimes by its Indian name, kit-kit-dizze. There are also several fine ponderosa pines along here; look for the pines with long needles growing in clusters of three.

At 1 mile the trail gains the ridge (elevation 7100 feet), turns in a northerly direction, and soon becomes almost level. You now enter a very dense forest of firs and lodgepole pines. Notice that almost no vegetation is growing in the dark shade of the forest floor. Under natural conditions, this plateau would have been set ablaze by lightning long ago, but our fire suppression policies of the past one hundred years have turned this area into an almost impenetrable thicket incapable of supporting a healthy variety of plants and wildlife. In recent years the Park Service has tried to establish a policy of allowing fires in areas such as this to burn when ignited by lightning.

As you begin to leave the dense forest, the trail climbs moderately through rocky switchbacks, and at 2 miles you cross the main fork of Silliman Creek, elevation 7600 feet. This creek drains about half of the Silliman Crest and, as you can see by the deep gorge it has cut for itself, there are times when it carries a considerable volume of water. When the water level is high, you must use extra caution when crossing here. Please note that Silliman Creek serves as the water supply for Lodgepole; camping, swimming, fishing and picnicking are not allowed here.

The trail now climbs steeply up the south-facing slope. Looking to the southeast, you have a view of Alta Peak.

At 2 1/2 miles you reach Cahoon Meadow, elevation 7800 feet. This is a lush, nearly flat meadow—the finest meadow a day hiker will see in the Lodgepole area. It's also a good place for spotting wildlife. If you approach the meadow quietly, you may see deer or bear. If Cahoon Meadow is your destination for the day, take a little time to walk around the meadow and enjoy its beautiful setting.

Throughout much of the Sierra Nevada, meadows have been heavily grazed by cattle and sheep for more than a hundred years. Even in the national parks, many backcountry meadows are grazed by pack stock. But Cahoon Meadow is an excellent example of what a meadow should look like in its natural state. Notice the serpentine pattern of the creek as it meanders slowly through the thick sedges. Meadows that have been heavily grazed often loose this serpentine pattern and end up with a swiftly-flowing creek which quickly erodes the meadow, eventually leading to its destruction.

As the trail circles around the upper end of Cahoon Meadow, it begins climbing steeply again. Looking to the north you can see the ridge you must gain to reach Cahoon Gap. You now cross several small creeks feeding into Cahoon Meadow, as you climb through the red fir forest.

After a long and steep climb, you reach Cahoon Gap, 4 1/4 miles, elevation 8650 feet. If you happen to be here in the fall, you will most likely hear the startling thud of red fir cones hitting the ground. Almost immediately, chipmunks rip the cones to shreds in search of the small seeds inside. Sometimes in the fall you will also find bear scat filled with the seeds from red fir cones.

The trail descends quickly to Clover Creek, 5 miles, elevation 8400 feet. There are several campsites along the creek here where you can rest and eat. This area is popular with fishermen, who fish both up and down Clover Creek. There is no trail downstream, but it is possible to follow the creek for a mile or so before the route becomes very rugged.

There is a trail that follows Clover Creek upstream (east) to Twin Lakes, 6 3/4 miles, elevation 9500 feet.

To the north a trail continues to JO Pass, 7 miles, elevation 9400 feet. The ridge at JO Pass is the boundary between Sequoia National Park and Sequoia National Forest. The pass (pronounced "jay-oh") acquired its unusual name when an early traveler, John Warren, carved the first two initials of his name on a tree there.

It's possible to make a long, one-way hike of this trail by continuing over JO Pass to Rowell Meadow (in Sequoia National Forest), and then to the Sunset Meadow trailhead, 11 miles, elevation 8000 feet, where you would have a car waiting for you. Better yet would be to have somebody drop you off at Sunset Meadow so you could then hike back to Lodgepole. To reach Sunset Meadow by car, drive north on the Generals Highway until you reach the Big Meadows Road; turn east and drive about 12 miles to the Sunset Meadow Road; turn south and drive 2 miles to the trailhead. Park visitor centers sell a map of Sequoia National Forest to help you find your way.

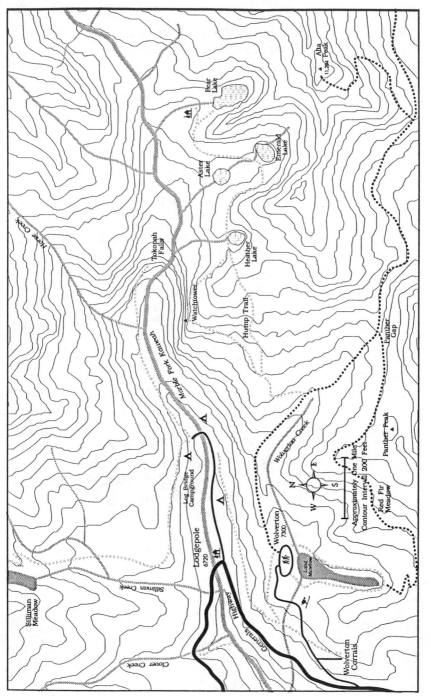

Alta Trail

ALTA TRAIL

DISTANCE: 2 3/4 Miles to Panther Gap, 5 3/4 Miles to Alta
Meadow
HIKING TIME: 3 Hours to Panther Gap, 6 Hours to Alta
Meadow
STARTING ELEVATION: 7300'
HIGHEST ELEVATION: 8400' at Panther Gap, 9250' at
Alta Meadow
DIFFICULTY: Strenuous
USGS MAP: Triple Divide

Although the Alta Trail really begins at Giant Forest Village, the
first two miles parallel the Generals Highway, and all the major points
of interest on that section of trail can be reached more conveniently by
other trails described in this guidebook. For the purpose of making a
day hike to Panther Gap or Alta Meadow, it makes more sense to start
at Wolverton, which is about 1000 feet higher than Giant Forest Village
and more than 3 miles closer to your destination.

Begin on the Lakes Trail, at the Wolverton parking area. As you
drive into the parking area, you'll see a sign directing you ,o the
trailhead at the northeast end of the parking area.

The trail heads north for just a few hundred feet, then turns to the
east, following the ridge between Lodgepole and Wolverton.

After about a mile, the trail begins turning to the southeast,
following the route of Wolverton Creek.

You cross a small unnamed creek with rocky banks and a scattering of aspens. Then, at 1 3/4 miles, you come to the junction of the
Panther Gap Trail, elevation 8000 feet. Here you leave the Lakes Trail
and head southeast, climbing steeply through the red-fir forest along
Wolverton Creek.

At 2 3/4 miles you reach the Alta Trail at Panther Gap, elevation
8400 feet, where you have an excellent view of the Great Western
Divide from Mt. Stewart to Mineral King. Looking south, across the
Middle Fork of the Kaweah, you can see Castle Rocks.

The name "panther," of course, is another name for the mountain lion, or cougar. This nocturnal animal covers a very large territory and preys almost entirely on deer. Though the lions are not endangered—in fact some people believe lion numbers have been increasing in recent years—they are seldom seen. There are park personnel who have worked in Sequoia for thirty years and never seen a mountain lion. Some park visitors, on the other hand, have been lucky enough to spot one on their first visit.

Continuing east on the Alta Trail, you climb the south-facing slope of what is really a ridge of Alta Peak. The red-fir forest becomes much less dense, and the landscape is dominated by chinquapin, ceanothus and manzanita. After 1/2 mile, looking back to the west, you can see the distinctive rock feature known as Panther Peak. Directly below you are the headwaters of Panther Creek. If you look carefully, you may see portions of the High Sierra Trail, 1600 feet below.

At 3 3/4 miles you come to the Seven-Mile Hill Trail. At one time this very steep trail descended all the way to the Middle Fork, though it's only maintained as far as the High Sierra Trail now.

A little farther on, looking to the east, you can see a portion of Alta Meadow, still 2 miles away. The rock feature above Alta Meadow is Tharp's Rock.

4 Miles brings you to Mehrten Meadow, where there's a small creek, as well as level campsites that make good rest areas. The Mehrtens were early settlers and cattlemen in Tulare County, though it isn't known which of the four Mehrten brothers this creek was named after.

At 4 3/4 miles you come to a metal sign marking the junction of the Alta Peak Trail, elevation 9150 feet. From this point it's still 2 miles and a 2000 foot elevation gain to Alta Peak. For most day hikers it would not be reasonable to attempt climbing Alta Peak and returning to Wolverton in a day. Still, a brief description is given here: (Turning north, you climb steeply on a maintained trail, contouring around and below Tharp's Rock. You then climb even more steeply, passing timberline at about 10,300 feet. You reach the summit of Alta peak at 11,204 feet.)

Taking the lower trail, an easy mile brings you to Alta Meadow, elevation 9250 feet. Because of its unusual ridge-top location, this meadow has outstanding views of the Great Western Divide.

On your return hike to Wolverton, it's possible to make a partial loop by adding a little more than a mile to your total distance. This route, given below, is interesting and strongly recommended:

Return to Panther Gap, then continue hiking west, staying on the Alta Trail rather than dropping down to Wolverton Creek. You contour around the north side of Panther Rock, climbing slightly for 1/2 mile until you reach Panther Meadow just above the trail.

The trail now begins dropping. If you're a tree buff, see if you can spot the western white pines, a five-needle pine similar to the sugar pine though not nearly as common.

The trail continues dropping steeply to Red Fir Meadow, elevation 8300 feet, 2 miles from Panther Gap. This quiet, seldom-visited meadow is a likely place to spot wildlife. Fingers of the meadow extend into the forest, and other parts are overgrown with willows.

After descending for another 1/2 mile, you come to a trail junction, elevation 7700 feet. Here you leave the Alta Trail and turn north, downhill.

The steep descent soon brings you to another trail junction. Continue straight ahead, north, following the less-worn trail. (The other trail (the well-worn trail to the east) will also take you to Wolverton but adds 1/4 mile to your hike.)

Descend to Long Meadow and follow the meadow's edge, resisting the temptation to cut across. Continue for 1/4 mile until you see a footpath turning east and following a culvert over Wolverton Creek. This returns you to the Wolverton parking area, a total of 4 miles from Panther Gap.

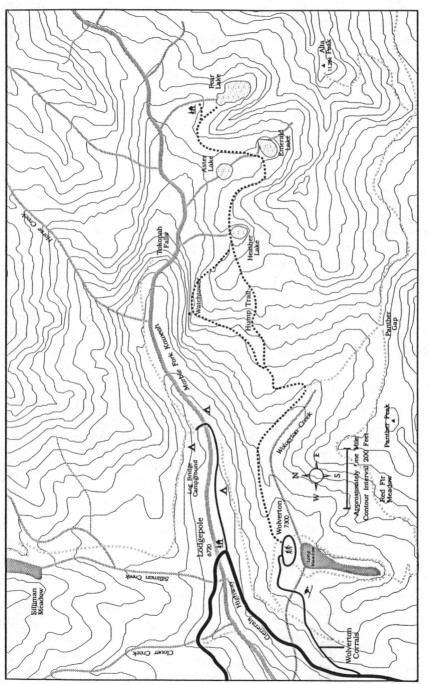

Lakes Trail

LAKES TRAIL

DISTANCE: 4 Miles to Heather Lake, 6 1/4 Miles to Pear
Lake
HIKING TIME: 3 Hours to Heather Lake, 5 Hours to Pear
Lake
STARTING ELEVATION: 7300′
HIGHEST ELEVATION: 9510′ at Pear Lake
DIFFICULTY: Strenuous
USGS MAP: Triple Divide

The Lakes Trail is the most popular short backpacking trip in Sequoia National Park. Not only is the trail very beautiful, but it offers a wonderful degree of diversity over just a few miles. Heavy overnight use has had a serious impact on the fragile areas around the lakes though, and just a few overnight backpackers are allowed onto the trail each day. With the trailhead quotas now in effect, most backpackers who would like to hike into the Emerald and Pear Lake areas cannot get wilderness permits. But wilderness permits are not required for day hikers, and many day hikers will find that the distances to the lakes, as well as the degrees of difficulty, are not beyond their ability. A fit hiker is perfectly capable of hiking to Pear Lake and back in a day. Some very fit hikers even continue on, climbing Alta Peak and returning to Wolverton by way of the Alta Trail. For less ambitious hikers, there are several worthy destinations along the Lakes Trail.

Begin the Lakes Trail at the Wolverton parking area. As you drive into the parking area, you'll see a sign directing you to the trailhead at the northeast end of the parking area.

The trail heads north for just a few hundred feet, then turns to the east, following the ridge between Lodgepole and Wolverton. Through the dense red firs you soon begin to see views of Tokopah to the northeast.

After about a mile the trail begins turning to the southeast, following the route of Wolverton Creek.

You cross a small unnamed creek with rocky banks and a scattering of aspens. Then, at 1 3/4 miles, you come to the junction of the Panther Gap Trail, elevation 8000 feet. Staying on the Pear Lake Trail, you switchback to the northeast (uphill).

At 2 miles you come to the junction of the Hump Trail and the Watchtower Trail. Here you have a decision to make. Both trails take you to Heather Lake and all points beyond. The Watchtower Trail is 1/2 mile longer, but the Hump Trail climbs 250 feet higher. The view from the Watchtower is spectacular, but the Hump Trail has its scenic merits as well. In the winter, spring, and sometimes in the early summer, portions of the Watchtower Trail can be icy and unsafe; you should avoid the Watchtower during those times. As a suggestion, take the Hump Trail now, and return by way of the Watchtower.

You only have to climb a few feet up the Hump Trail to know how it got its name; in the next mile or so you gain more than 1100 feet in elevation. You soon begin to emerge from the dense red-fir forest and enter a rocky subalpine terrain. At about 3 1/2 miles, elevation 9450 feet, you reach the summit of the Hump. To the east, the open rocky area that reaches to the skyline is known as the Tableland. A cross-country route over the Tableland provides backpackers with a shortcut into Deadman Canyon and the Roaring River country. In the winter, the Tableland becomes a popular playground for cross-country skiers.

You descend a few steep switchbacks until you come to a junction at the east end of the Watchtower Trail, 3 3/4 miles. This is the route you will take on your return journey. For the time being, however, continue to the east until you come to Heather Lake, 4 miles, elevation 9200 feet. This lovely little lake takes its name from the red heather which can be found growing along its banks.

As you begin climbing the low ridge east of Heather Lake, you begin to see foxtail pines, with thick orange bark and bushy branches. These hardy trees only grow at high elevations and can tolerate very cold temperatures, heavy snowfall and intense winds. The great character of their twisted limbs has become a kind of symbol of the High Sierra.

You descend the east side of the ridge to Emerald Lake, 5 1/4 miles, elevation 9200 feet. Above the lake you can see the summit of Alta Peak. Aster Lake is just 1/4 mile to the north, in the same drainage as Emerald Lake.

You might be curious about the high-tech outhouse at Emerald Lake. This is a compost toilet which uses electricity from a photovoltaic panel to heat the organic waste and speed its decomposition. In this cold environment, buried waste decomposes very slowly. (As a research project, the Sierra Club once unearthed old latrines in the High Sierra and found that almost no decomposition had taken place.) Hauling the waste out by mule or helicopter is very expensive, so perhaps a photovoltaic outhouse is the solution.

From the campsites at Emerald Lake, the trail veers north and begins climbing the ridge, exposing views of the Silliman Crest to the north. A little farther on, looking west, you can see the Watchtower, which overlooks Tokopah Valley.

As you reach the top of the ridge separating Emerald Lake and Pear Lake, you come to a junction. The Pear Lake Ranger Station is to the northeast 1/4 mile; during the summer months a ranger is stationed there. Pear Lake itself is to the southeast 1/2 mile.

Taking the right fork to the lake, you contour around the rocky point of the ridge and climb until you reach Pear Lake, surrounded by a backdrop of sheer granite cliffs. The summit of Alta Peak, elevation 11,204 feet is to the southeast.

On your return, you may want to go by way of the ranger station. There is no trail, but follow the outlet of Pear Lake, staying on the west side of the creek, for 1/4 mile. After descending 300 feet in elevation, look for the Pear Lake Ranger Station, elevation 9200 feet, in a cluster of trees beside the creek. This sturdy building of granite, with timber rafters and shake-shingle roof, is the most beautiful of all the backcountry stations in Sequoia. It was built by the Civilian Conservation Corps in 1940. During the winter it is available, on a reservation basis, for cross-country skiers. For more information, contact the Sequoia Natural History Association, Ash Mountain, Box 10, Three Rivers, CA 93271.

From the ranger station a trail heads west 1/2 mile, climbing moderately, before rejoining the main trail.

To hike the Watchtower Trail on your way back to Wolverton, return to Heather Lake and continue following the trail for a few hundred feet until you see the metal trail sign which reads, "Wolverton Via Watchtower." Remember, the Watchtower Trail can be unsafe in the winter, spring and early summer. Do not take this route if there are patches of snow on the trail beyond this point.

The Watchtower Trail was built by the Civilian Conservation Corps in 1935. Much of the trail had to be blasted out of the cliff side; in other places rock riprap was used to build up a trail bed. If heights make you nervous, this isn't the route to take. Most hikers, though, will be thrilled by the sheer 1600-foot drop off, and by the breathtaking view of Tokopah Valley and Tokopah Falls below.

The trail follows to the south of the Watchtower itself, which is a rocky pinnacle extending out from the cliff side. It is possible to climb to the pinnacle by continuing down the trail (west) two switchbacks, until you see a rough footpath which climbs back up a rock ledge to the summit of the Watchtower. Be extremely cautious here.

Leaving the Watchtower, the trail makes one long traverse down the west-facing slope until it reaches the junction of the Hump Trail. You now return to Wolverton parking area by the same route you hiked earlier.

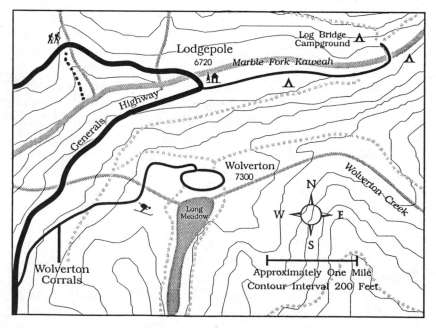

Clover Creek Footpath

CLOVER CREEK FOOTPATH

DISTANCE: 1/2 Mile (one way)
HIKING TIME: 1/2 Hour (return trip longer)
STARTING ELEVATION: 6800′
LOWEST ELEVATION: 6400′
DIFFICULTY: Strenuous
USGS MAP: Triple Divide

This short but rugged hike is for experienced hikers only. The footpath is not maintained and is steep and strenuous. It is not suitable for hikers with young children, and it is not suitable for any hikers in the spring and early summer when the water level is high and the rocks slippery. It is described here only as an alternative fishing spot for hardy fishermen looking for a route down to the Marble Fork. Though the area at the confluence of Clover Creek and the Marble Fork is attractive, all hikers should use this area with extreme caution.

The footpath begins at the Clover Creek Bridge, on the Generals Highway, 1 mile west of Lodgepole. There is a small parking area on the south side of the road, just west of the bridge.

DO NOT follow the rocky area along Clover Creek itself. Descend through the wooded area on the west side of the creek, staying at least one hundred feet from the creek. There is a faint fisherman's path, but this may be hard to follow at times.

After descending 1/2 mile, you come to the confluence of Clover Creek and the Marble Fork of the Kaweah, where there are pools for fishing. Though there is no trail, it's possible to walk a short ways down the Marble Fork, keeping in mind that this area is steep and rugged, and the slippery rocks can be very treacherous.

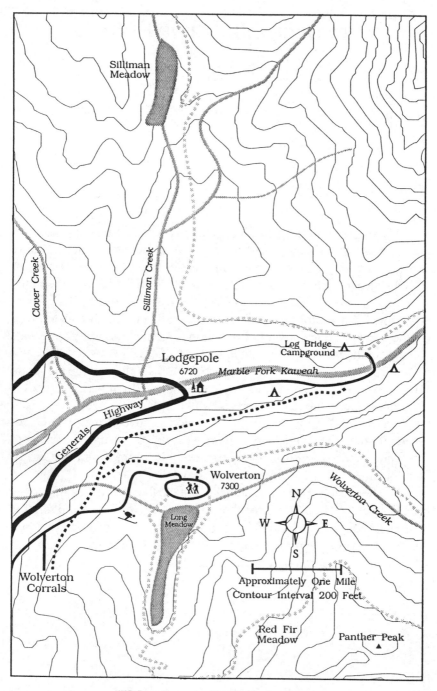

Silliman Meadow

Clover Creek

Silliman Creek

Log Bridge Campground

Lodgepole
6720   Marble Fork Kaweah

Highway

Generals

Wolverton
7300

Long Meadow

Wolverton Creek

N
W   E
S

Wolverton Corrals

Approximately One Mile
Contour Interval 200 Feet

Red Fir Meadow

Panther Peak

Wolverton to Lodgepole Trail

WOLVERTON to LODGEPOLE TRAIL

DISTANCE: 1 1/2 Miles (one way)
HIKING TIME: 1 Hour (one way)
STARTING ELEVATION: 7300'
LOWEST ELEVATION: 6800'
DIFFICULTY: Easy
USGS MAP: Triple Divide

This short trail is useful for hikers who have been on the Lakes Trail or Alta Trail and want to hike back to Lodgepole. Or, if you have children, it's fun to take them to the Wolverton Corrals to see the horses, then walk back to Lodgepole.

There are at least two ways to start this trail. One is to begin at the Wolverton parking area. As you drive into the parking area, you see a sign directing you to the trailhead at the northeast end of the parking area. Follow the Lakes Trail north for just a few hundred feet, then turn to the west at the top of the ridge. You hike downhill for 1/2 mile, where you then strike the main fork of this trail. Turn north (right) and continue downhill for 1 mile to Lodgepole campground.

The second way to start this trail is from the Wolverton Road, 0.6 miles from the Generals Highway. Here you see a painted crosswalk and, on the north side of the Wolverton Road, a small trail sign which reads, "Lodgepole 1.6."

The trail is more or less level for the first 1/2 mile, where you reach Wolverton Creek. You cross the creek on a culvert bridge, then continue downhill for about 1 mile to Lodgepole campground.

As you can see, this trail was once a road. Before the Generals Highway was opened in 1926, this was the only road from Wolverton to Lodgepole. For the last seventy years or so, this trail has been used mostly by black bears traveling from their last meal at Wolverton parking area to their next meal at Lodgepole campground.

(Note: You can also begin at Wolverton Corrals. From the east end of the corrals, hike north on the dirt road 1/4 mile to the Wolverton Road and the trailhead described above.)

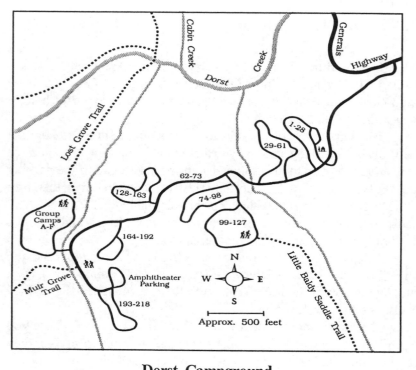

Dorst Campground

Introduction to Dorst Creek

Dorst Creek was named after Captain Joseph Dorst, the first superintendent of Sequoia National Park. A cavalryman and graduate of West Point, Dorst took control of the park in May of 1891, just a few months after Congress passed the legislation establishing it. His first duties were to protect the park from loggers, poachers, sheepherders and cattlemen, but during the years of his control his soldiers also helped build some of the park's roads and trails.

For many years Dorst campground has been one of the most popular campgrounds in the park. Dorst Creek, a beautiful medium-size stream, is a big attraction in itself. But there are also a couple of very nice trails which begin at the campground. The Muir Grove Trail in particular rates as one of the best trails for viewing majestic, undisturbed giant sequoias in this park.

Almost every year there's a search for a lost camper in the Dorst Creek area. Perhaps this is because Dorst campground, with its easy accessibility, attracts so many first-time campers. But the terrain around Dorst Creek must also be partly to blame. The area is heavily wooded, and it's sometimes difficult to fix your bearings on distant landmarks here. Once you become disoriented, the terrain all looks remarkably alike—mostly dense stands of red and white firs. Unless you're very familiar with this area, or you're an accomplished route finder, be sure to stay on the trails while hiking in the Dorst Creek area.

Officially all trails from Dorst campground begin at the amphitheater, but it may be more convenient for you to pick up the trail at the point where it leaves the camp perimeter. Using each trail description, as well as the map of Dorst campground on page 138, you will be able to find that point.

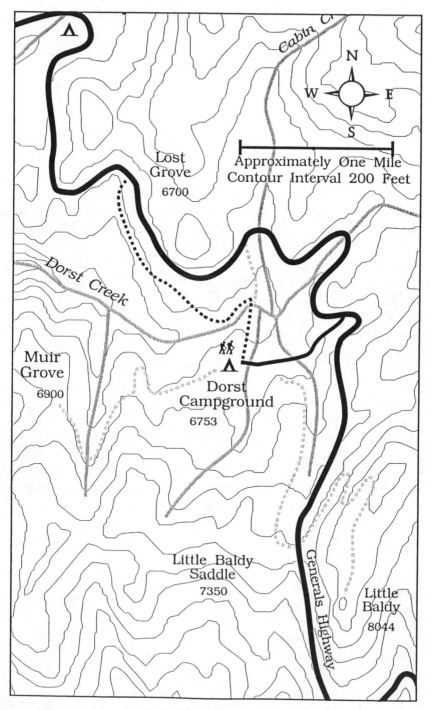

Lost Grove Trail

LOST GROVE TRAIL

DISTANCE: 2 1/2 Miles (one way)
HIKING TIME: 2 Hours (one way)
STARTING ELEVATION: 6753'
LOWEST ELEVATION: 6500' (Dorst Creek)
DIFFICULTY: Moderate
USGS MAP: Giant Forest

Although it's possible to drive to Lost Grove from Dorst campground, everyone staying at the campground should try this short trail at least once. In the spring or fall, when the campground is closed, this trail takes you over a quiet corner of the park where you aren't likely to see another soul.

You'll find the trailhead in the group camp area, at the northeast end of parking area B. (See the map on page 139.)

You begin by following a fork of Dorst Creek, on the west side of the creek, hiking north, downhill.

At 1/2 mile you come to the main fork of Dorst Creek. This makes a fine destination if you're hiking with young children. There are pools along the creek to play in, and shady places among the willows to have a picnic. Use caution here in the spring and early summer when the water level is high.

You now cross Dorst Creek, where there is no bridge, and pick up the trail again on the other side.

Just two hundred feet from Dorst Creek you come to a trail junction. The trail to the right (north) leads you up Cabin Creek to the Generals Highway, 1/2 mile. (See page 145 for a description of that trail). The trail to the left (west) leads you to Lost Grove.

For the next mile you traverse the south-facing slope above Dorst Creek. At one point the trail drops about 100 feet in elevation to avoid a large rock outcropping, so watch carefully to find the trail there.

As you pass through the thick forest of white firs, notice the heavy accumulation of downed trees and limbs—forest litter it's called. Under natural conditions this area would have been burned in a lightning-caused fire long ago. Now the firs have so dominated the forest canopy that almost no other species of plant is able to grow. This area is a prime candidate for a prescribed burn, which would clean up the forest floor and open the canopy.

Through the trees to the west you can catch occasional glimpses of Big Baldy and Chimney Rock, both outside the park.

At 1 1/4 miles you cross a small, unnamed drainage with willows and ferns growing along it.

1 1/2 miles brings you to a small meadow thick with lupine. Various species of this highly adaptable plant grow from South America to Alaska, and in California alone there are more than sixty different species of lupine. It's a nitrogen-fixing legume; with the help of bacteria which live on its roots, it's able to take nitrogen from the air and return it to the soil. This ability is beneficial to the surrounding plants, which need nitrogen in the soil in order to grow. The lupine seeds, which look almost like green beans, are said to be poisonous for cattle and horses, though the Indians apparently ate them in great numbers.

You now cross two drainages feeding this meadow. If you look uphill after crossing the second drainage, you can see giant sequoias in the lower end of Lost Grove. Don't be fooled by the very large cedars which are also growing on the fringes of Lost Grove.

The trail now turns in a more northerly direction and begins climbing steeply.

At 2 miles you come to a trail junction. The trail to the left (west) takes you to the park boundary, 1/2 mile, and to Stony Creek, about 1 1/2 miles. The trail to the right (north) leads you to Lost Grove.

You now pass through the heart of Lost Grove, a fine stand of large sequoias, and make one last steep climb to the Generals Highway and the Lost Grove parking area, elevation 6700 feet.

When the Generals Highway first opened in 1926, King Canyon, to the north of Sequoia, was not yet a national park. (That didn't come until 1940.) At that time, Sequoia's northern entrance station was here at Lost Grove.

Part of Lost Grove continues on the hillside above the highway.

You can return to Dorst campground by way of the trail you just hiked, or better yet you can follow the shoulder of the highway south about 1 mile to Cabin Creek. The trail there, described on page 145, returns you to Dorst Creek and Dorst campground.

Sugar Pine Bark

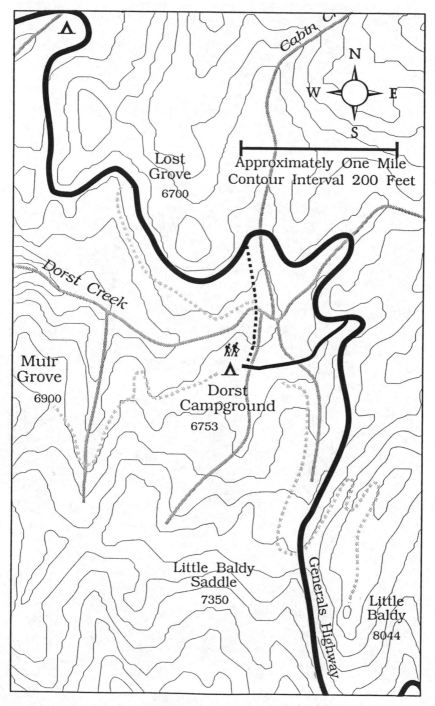

Cabin Creek Trail

CABIN CREEK TRAIL

DISTANCE: 1 Mile (one way)
HIKING TIME: 1/2 Hour (one way)
STARTING ELEVATION: 6700'
LOWEST ELEVATION: 6500' (Dorst Creek)
DIFFICULTY: Easy
USGS MAP: Giant Forest

This is a fun little trail for hikers who can only bear the thought of traveling downhill. By the time they get to the bottom maybe they'll have enough oxygen flowing to their brain they'll be inspired to try something more challenging. If you happen to be staying at Dorst campground, you might have somebody drop you off at Cabin Creek, on the Generals Highway, then walk back to camp. Or you might use this as a way to return to Dorst campground after hiking to Lost Grove.

The trail begins on the Generals Highway where Cabin Creek crosses the highway, 1.5 miles northwest of Dorst campground. There's a small, unpaved turnout on the south side of the highway, west of Cabin Creek.

You'll find the trail just below the turnout. It follows the course of Cabin Creek, staying in the woods the entire way. Though this trail is not often maintained by park trail crews, its path is very old and fairly easy to follow. You may have to scramble over a few downed trees here and there.

At 1/2 mile you come to Dorst Creek, where there are good pools for swimming and fishing. Cross to the south side, using caution in the spring and early summer when the water level is high, then follow the trail up the small fork of Dorst Creek to Dorst campground, elevation 6753 feet.

If you want to hike this trail in the other direction, traveling from Dorst campground to the Generals Highway, simply follow the Lost Grove trail for the first half mile or so until you cross Dorst Creek.

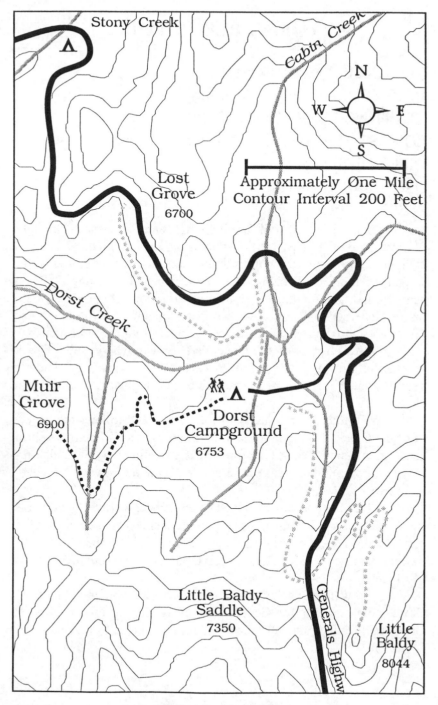

Stony Creek

Cabin Creek

N
W   E
S

Lost
Grove
6700

Approximately One Mile
Contour Interval 200 Feet

Dorst Creek

Muir
Grove
6900

Dorst
Campground
6753

Little Baldy
Saddle
7350

Generals Highw

Little
Baldy
8044

Muir Grove Trail

MUIR GROVE TRAIL

DISTANCE: 2 Miles (one way)
HIKING TIME: 1 1/2 Hours (one way)
STARTING ELEVATION: 6753'
HIGHEST ELEVATION: 6900'
DIFFICULTY: Moderate
USGS MAP: Giant Forest

The Muir Grove Trail goes unseen by most visitors to Sequoia simply because the trailhead is tucked away in Dorst campground and not all that easy to find. Yet it's one of the finest trails for seeing an undisturbed grove of sequoias and easy enough to be enjoyed by almost all hikers.

You'll find the Muir Grove trailhead in Dorst campground between the group camp area and the amphitheater parking lot, on the west side of the road. Once you've located the trailhead sign, it's best to park at the nearby amphitheater and walk back. (See the map of Dorst campground on page 138.)

The trail begins by following the south side of a small meadow, heading in a westerly direction. As you begin to traverse a forested hillside, you can see the Dorst Creek drainage to the north.

At 1/2 mile you cross a steep creek with a slick, rock bed. The trail continues to climb moderately, making just two switchbacks, until at 1 mile you reach a large granite dome. From here you have an excellent view of the Dorst and Stony Creek drainages to the north, and just a glimpse of Chimney Rock. The point at which Dorst Creek meets Stony Creek is considered the head of the North Fork of the Kaweah, but that's very rugged country and there are no trails leading there. Looking toward the ridge to the west, you can see the large sequoias of Muir Grove. If you're hiking this trail in the summer, the view to the west and slightly below you is probably smoggy. In fact, smog drifting in from the urban areas of California is the single greatest threat to Sequoia National Park. About one third of the trees in Sequoia show some smog-caused damage. The damage is most visible in a mottling of the trees' leaves and needles. Obviously that mottling will have some effect on the trees' ability to convert sunlight into stored energy, but whether or not the trees of Sequoia can survive that kind of damage over a long period of time is unknown.

The trail descends slightly until you cross another small fork of Dorst Creek at 1 1/2 miles.

You now climb moderately until you gain the ridge top and reach Muir Grove, elevation 6900 feet, named after the great mountain tramp John Muir.

During the summer of 1875, Muir made a leisurely trek through the belt of sequoias in what is now Sequoia and Kings Canyon National Parks. Muir was an amateur botanist and an excellent observer of nature, and by the end of that summer he knew more about giant sequoias than anyone alive. His account of his journey through the sequoia groves not only added to the scientific knowledge of the time, but raised some important questions about the long-term preservation of the sequoias. Even at that early date the redwoods were being cut down as quickly as the tools and technology of the time would allow, and almost nobody spoke of the giant sequoias as a limited resource which must be protected. Because of his concern and great vision for the future, John Muir has to be considered the grandfather of California's national parks.

Spend a few minutes walking around Muir Grove. It has a magic and charm which only a remote sequoia grove can have.

There's an old trail, not maintained in several years, which continues down the west-facing slope to Skagway Grove, Hidden Springs, and even as far as the North Fork of the Kaweah. That trail is very rugged, brushy, difficult to follow, and is not suitable for most day hikers.

Great Western Divide

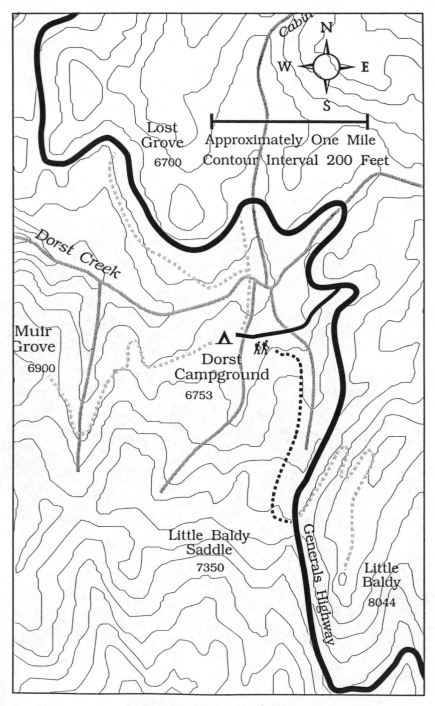

Little Baldy Saddle Trail

LITTLE BALDY SADDLE TRAIL

DISTANCE: 1 1/2 Miles (one way)
HIKING TIME: 1 Hour (one way)
STARTING ELEVATION: 6753'
HIGHEST ELEVATION: 7350'
DIFFICULTY: Moderate
USGS MAP: Giant Forest

Though this trail is steeper than most hikers would like, and not particularly scenic, it's included here as a hiking route to the Little Baldy trailhead. Using this trail, it's possible to begin at Dorst campground, hike all the way to Little Baldy, and return to the campground without using your car. Or you might have somebody drop you off at Little Baldy Saddle, climb Little Baldy, then use this trail as a route back to Dorst campground. (See page 153 for a description of the Little Baldy Trail.)

The trail begins in Dorst campground near campsite 120. (See the map of Dorst campground on page 138.) There's a small parking area nearby. Look for a sign which reads, "Walk-in Sites 118—120." Just east of the parking area you'll find a dirt road. Follow the road uphill 1/4 mile to a water tank. To the right (west) of the water tank you'll see a sign marking the trailhead.

The trail heads in a southerly direction, following on the west side of a small fork of Dorst Creek. It climbs steeply for 1/4 mile, then levels off to moderately steep.

After climbing through a dense forest of white firs, at 1 1/4 miles you gain the ridgetop. Here the trail turns north and soon brings you to the Generals Highway and Little Baldy Saddle, elevation 7350 feet. To the east you see the dome of Little Baldy. The Little Baldy Trail begins directly across the highway.

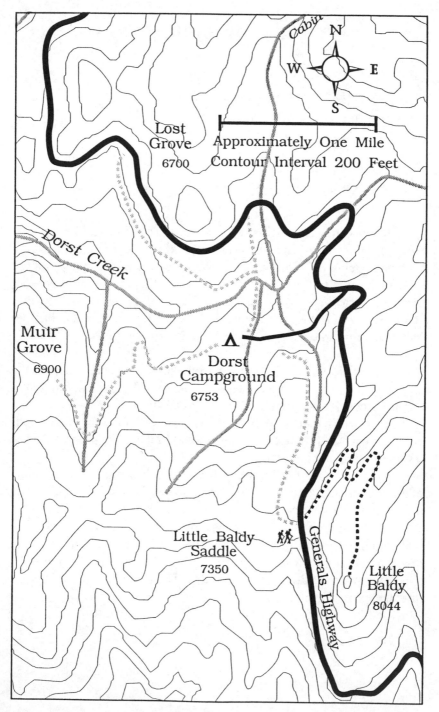

Little Baldy Trail

LITTLE BALDY TRAIL

DISTANCE: 1 3/4 Miles (one way)
HIKING TIME: 1 Hour (one way)
STARTING ELEVATION: 7350'
HIGHEST ELEVATION: 8050'
DIFFICULTY: Moderate
USGS MAP: Giant Forest

This trail offers one of the finest views of any day hike in Sequoia National Park. If you've been hiking in the heavily-forested sequoia groves, you'll find this hike to be a refreshing change. For an added thrill, you might consider hiking this trail on a full moon or on a starry night.

The trail begins at Little Baldy Saddle, on the Generals Highway, 6.6 miles northwest of Lodgepole, or 1.5 miles south of Dorst campground. There's a small but well-marked parking area at the saddle, and the trailhead is on the east side of the road.

You can also reach this trailhead from Dorst campground by way of the Little Baldy Saddle Trail described on page 151. If you're staying at Dorst campground, you might want to have somebody drop you off at Little Baldy Saddle, climb Little Baldy, then hike back to Dorst campground.

The trail begins by climbing moderately steep switchbacks. Through the red firs to the west you can see Little Baldy's cousin, Big Baldy, and in front of that a peculiar rock formation called Chimney Rock. Both are in Sequoia National Forest.

As you climb a little higher you see Dorst Creek to the west and, beyond that, Stony Creek.

After hiking 1 1/4 miles, at an elevation of about 8000 feet, you gain the ridge top. From this point on the trail is nearly level.

Notice how the red firs here almost totally dominate the forest. Red firs are able to tolerate shade better than the pines, and therefore thrive on cool, north-facing slopes such as this.

From the summit of Little Baldy, you enjoy a panorama unlike any other in the park. To the east is the crest of the Great Western Divide, and to the southeast you can see Mineral King Valley and nearly all of Farewell Gap. To the west is a corner of the park rarely seen from any other vantage point: Yucca Creek, Cave Creek, and even the upper North Fork of the Kaweah. At one time, many years ago, there was a network of trails through that region of the park, but the trails haven't been maintained and, as you can see, the brush has grown very thick, making most of that area inaccessible.

Keep in mind that there is the potential for injury by lightning on Little Baldy. If there are dark clouds nearby, thunder, hail, rain, or if you hear or feel static electricity in the air, descend from the summit and find shelter.

The summit of Little Baldy is sometimes used as an overnight camping spot. The view of the starry sky is exceptional, and watching the sun come up over the Great Western Divide is equally enjoyable. Remember, though, that if you spend the night on Little Baldy you must obtain an overnight wilderness permit at the Lodgepole ranger station. Be sure to carry plenty of water—none is found on or near the summit.

Introduction to Mineral King

and

Atwell Mill

Although Mineral King didn't become part of Sequoia National Park until 1978, in terms of the quality and beauty of its natural resources it has always been considered fine enough to be part of the park. It was Mineral King's unusual history as a mining district that kept it from being included in the park until such a late date.

Almost from the first time a white man set eyes on the Mineral King Valley, in 1862, the valley has been at the center of somebody's scheme to strike it rich. Throughout the 1870s, '80s and '90s, the favored scheme was mining for gold and silver. Although there was some gold and silver ore to be found in Mineral King, looking at the prospects now with an objective eye, it's obvious there was never enough ore to justify mining in that rugged and remote location. As with most frontier mining towns, it was the merchants and not the miners who struck it rich.

Most of the miners in Mineral King were also farmers and ranchers in Tulare County. Although Tulare County has always been a prosperous farming area, the citizens of the county couldn't help but dream of the great mining riches and economic boom which had come to communities in the Mother Lode area of California following the gold rush of 1848. Most of the citizens heartily believed that a great mining discovery would one day be made in the southern Sierra, and that it was only the extreme ruggedness of these mountains which had concealed the riches so far. But the truth was, and still remains, there are no significant gold or silver deposits in the southern Sierra Nevada between the San Joaquin River and White River. If gold had been discovered on the Kings or Kaweah, Sequoia and Kings Canyon National Parks probably never would have come into existence. We are fortunate today that nature spared us the greed and environmental devastation of a really big gold rush in the southern Sierra Nevada. But in Visalia in 1870, a person would have been lynched from an oak tree for speaking such thoughts.

There were ambitious schemes in the 1890s for logging the giant sequoias at Atwell Grove. The lumber mill at Atwell supplied the lumber for the mines, as well as for the hotels, cabins and stores of the original town at Mineral King, known then as Beulah. But the problem of transporting the lumber to the big markets in the San Joaquin Valley was insurmountable. Still, a great number of giant sequoias were cut down. In 1897 giant sequoias were turned into a million board feet of lumber for a flume that ran from Oak Grove to a hydroelectric plant at Hammond, just above Three Rivers.

Between 1904 and 1905, the company that built the hydroelectric plant, Mount Whitney Power, also built dams at the outlets of four Mineral King lakes—Monarch, Crystal, Franklin and Eagle—to regulate the flow of water into the flume. Even the miners of Mineral King considered that to be an environmental outrage.

By the turn of the century though, the mining boom had mostly gone bust, and more and more it seemed that Mineral King's future would be as a resort. The great earthquake of 1906, the same earthquake that destroyed San Francisco, triggered snow avalanches that leveled most of the buildings in Mineral King. But the town rebuilt and developed into a modest resort town.

As early as the 1890s, conservationists had hopes of incorporating Mineral King into Sequoia National Park. But those dreams were always defeated by the mining interests, the resort interests, the cattle and sheep grazing interests, and the logging interests. But it wasn't until after World War Two, when skiing became a major recreational sport in the United States, that Mineral King was threatened with really big-scale development. In 1965 the Walt Disney Corporation became interested in the idea of turning the valley into a huge ski complex that would serve as many as 10,000 skiers per day. After studying the area, ski experts declared that Mineral King could become the largest and finest alpine ski resort in the world. And with the eager compliance of the U.S. Forest Service, it appeared for several years as if that fate was inevitable.

What saved Mineral King from becoming a ski resort were the huge costs of building an all-weather road to the valley, revised estimates of the threat of snow avalanches, and, most of all, the environmental movement of the 1970s. After a long and bitter battle between developers and environmentalists, Mineral King became part of Sequoia National Park in 1978.

Today, hikers in Mineral King will find that many of the trails leading into the beautiful canyons surrounding the valley are steeper than most other trails in the park. Many of the trails began as rough access routes to the mines tucked back in the side canyons. In their eagerness to strike it rich, the miners saw no point in building elaborate trails and never imagined their routes would end up being used entirely by recreational hikers. Over the years, forest service and park service trails crews have improved the old mining routes, but the trails in Mineral King will probably always be a little steeper than we might like.

Because the routes are so direct, you'll cover fewer miles in Mineral King than in some other areas of the park, but you will have to work harder to do it. Keeping that in mind, hike a bit slower than you usually do and stop more often to take satisfaction in your progress.

The elevation at Mineral King Valley, 7500 feet, is high enough that most visitors will feel some effects of the altitude: shortness of breath, loss of energy, perhaps occasional headaches. The body's adjustment to high altitude, or "acclimatization," as it's called, takes about two weeks, though most of that process occurs in the first seventy-two hours. Hikers should remember to take it easy for the first few days they are here, and make their first hikes short ones.

Every year there are far too many accidents on the road to Mineral King. Much of the road is only wide enough for one vehicle, yet many people drive it as if the last thing in the world they expected to see was another car. Please drive the Mineral King Road as if you know for certain there is another car coming around every curve. Stay as far to the right as is safely possible and go slowly enough that you could stop at any time.

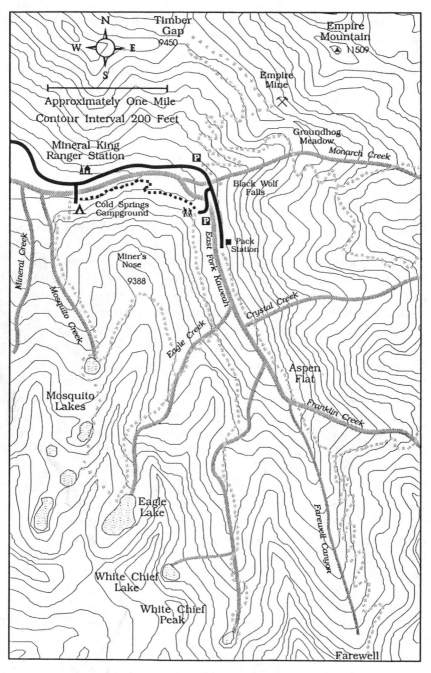

Cold Springs Trail

COLD SPRINGS TRAIL

DISTANCE: 1 Mile (one way)
HIKING TIME: 45 Minutes (one way)
STARTING ELEVATION: 7850'
LOWEST ELEVATION: 7500'
DIFFICULTY: Easy
USGS MAP: Mineral King

This short hike is just right for your first day in Mineral King. The trail is all downhill, and the distance is perfect for young children. If you only want to hike this trail one way, you might have somebody drop you off at the Eagle-Mosquito parking area and pick you up at Cold Springs campground.

The trail begins at the north end of the Eagle-Mosquito parking area, 1.2 miles south of the Mineral King ranger station.

For the first few hundred feet you pass through a cluster of cabins in an area which is part of the original settlement of Mineral King, known in the 1870s as "Beulah," the biblical land of promise. In 1870 there were 500 people living here, and dozens of gold and silver mines were being worked throughout the Mineral King area. By 1879, at the peak of the mining frenzy, there were said to be almost as many people living in Beulah as were living in Visalia, which at that time was the largest town in the southern San Joaquin Valley. The settlement was completely leveled by snow avalanches set off by the great earthquake of 1906, the same earthquake that destroyed San Francisco, and Beulah never regained its glory.

The trail approaches the East Fork of the Kaweah at about 1/2 mile. There are several places along here suitable for fishing and wading, as well as several pretty spots for a picnic.

At 3/4 miles you come to a self-guided nature trail which identifies some of the plants in Mineral King Valley, as well as the site of an old mine.

At 1 mile you reach Cold Springs campground, elevation 7500 feet.

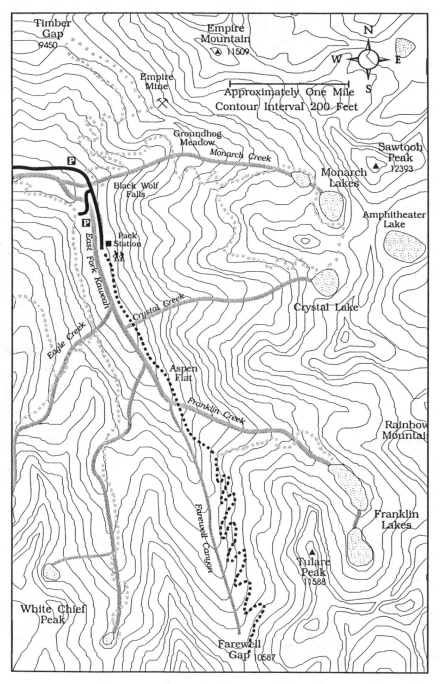

Farewell Gap Trail

FAREWELL GAP TRAIL

DISTANCE: 1 Mile to Aspen Flat, 5 1/2 Miles to Farewell Gap
HIKING TIME: Three Hours to Farewell Gap
STARTING ELEVATION: 7850′
HIGHEST ELEVATION: 10,587′
DIFFICULTY: Easy to Aspen Flat, Strenuous to Farewell Gap
USGS MAP: Mineral King

The first mile of this trail is nearly flat and very easy hiking, making it one of the best trails in Mineral King for young children, as well as one of the best trails for any hiker's first day at elevation. Also, there are several places along the first mile where you can stop to enjoy the river.

The Farewell Gap Trail begins at the south end of the Mineral King pack station, on the east side of the river. From the Mineral King ranger station drive east 1 mile, then begin looking for a parking place among the three turnouts along the road. You may not park along the dirt road leading into the pack station, nor at the pack station itself. If the turnouts are all taken, continue across the bridge and park at the Eagle-Mosquito parking area, then walk back to the trailhead at the south end of the corrals.

This trail is frequently used by pack stock. Please remember that the proper trail etiquette is for hikers to step off the trail on the downhill side and stand quietly until the pack stock have passed.

The trail follows the East Fork of the Kaweah. Notice the young juniper trees on the east side of the trail, the quaking aspens and the stands of red fir. But notice also that much of the slopes above Mineral King are open and clear of trees. Ordinarily at this elevation, the mountain slopes would be covered with conifers—mostly red firs. But the many snow avalanches that occur here in the winter have periodically swept the slopes free of trees, creating the beautiful subalpine look for which Mineral King is famous.

Look for patches of currants, with their bright red berries. Currants are one species of Ribes, a host plant in the life cycle of blister rust, a fungus that is threatening to wipe out sugar pines and other five-needle pines in the Sierra Nevada.

As you can see, much of Mineral King Valley is covered by a silvery sage. Because of its strong and distinctive aroma, the Indians often rubbed their bodies with this sage before hunting as a way to mask their scent.

Watchful hikers will probably see deer along the Farewell Gap Trail, either in the meadows and willows along the river, or on the slopes above the trail. If you aren't lucky enough to spot a deer, look for their arrow-shaped tracks in the soft dirt along the trail. Mineral King is almost perfect summer deer habitat. During the summer, the canyons surrounding the valley probably shelter more deer per square mile than any place in the southern Sierra. In the winter, conditions in Mineral King are too harsh for deer, so they migrate to lower elevations. Because the Park Service owns very little land at lower elevations, and because so much of the foothills surrounding the park are being developed, the problem of winter habitat for deer and other animals is becoming a critical one.

The first water crossing you come to is Crystal Creek, 3/4 miles, elevation 7950 feet. It drains from beautiful Crystal Lake, some 3000 feet above you.

Just past Crystal Creek you see an unmaintained footpath branching off to the southwest. If you choose to take this detour, it will lead you down to Aspen Flat, where there are pleasant places to rest or picnic in the shade. Aspen Flat is a good destination for those hiking with young children.

Beyond Crystal Creek, the trail begins climbing moderately. Look for wild cherry, a shrub-like plant with silvery bark and bright red fruit. These are sometimes known as "chokecherries," and if you sample the fruit you'll know why.

At 1 1/2 miles you come to Franklin Creek, elevation 8450 feet, named after John Crabtree's Lady Franklin Mine, which is farther up Franklin Canyon. There are places by the creek to rest or have lunch.

Beyond Franklin Creek the trail becomes more steep, with many short switchbacks. It's hard going now for the next hour.

At about 3 1/2 miles you come to the junction of the Franklin Lakes Trail, elevation 9300 feet. The Farewell Gap Trail continues climbing to the south, up one long switchback followed by several short ones. Notice how hikers have cut the switchbacks coming down from Farewell Gap and how their tracks have caused deeply-eroded ruts in the mountainside. As you can see, this is a very destructive practice that causes great harm. Please don't cut switchbacks.

At 5 1/2 miles you reach Farewell Gap, elevation 10,587 feet, with one of the finest views in Mineral King. As you look back into Mineral King Valley, the view you are seeing is the same view Harry Parole saw in the summer of 1862. Parole (also known as Harry O'Farrell) was hunting deer for the men working on the Hockett Trail across the Sierra. He rode to the top of Farewell Gap by way of the Little Kern, accompanied by a Paiute Indian whose name has gone unrecorded. Though Parole was the first white man to see Mineral King, it was of course well known to the local Indians. The Wukchumni, a band of Yokuts who spent their winters along the lower Kaweah River, migrated to what is now called Atwell Mill every summer.

To the south of you is Little Kern Canyon, and farther to the southeast you can see part of the lower Kern River Canyon, both outside the boundaries of the park. In the early days of Sequoia National Park, the heart of the backcountry (Kern River and the Kern Plateau) was reached by way of Farewell Gap and Coyote Pass, some ten miles to the southeast. Later, a more direct route by way of Franklin Pass was developed. Today Farewell Gap isn't used by backcountry travelers nearly as much as it once was, except in years of heavy snowfall. Then Franklin Pass is blocked with ice and snow until late in the summer and Farewell Gap again becomes the best route into the Kern River.

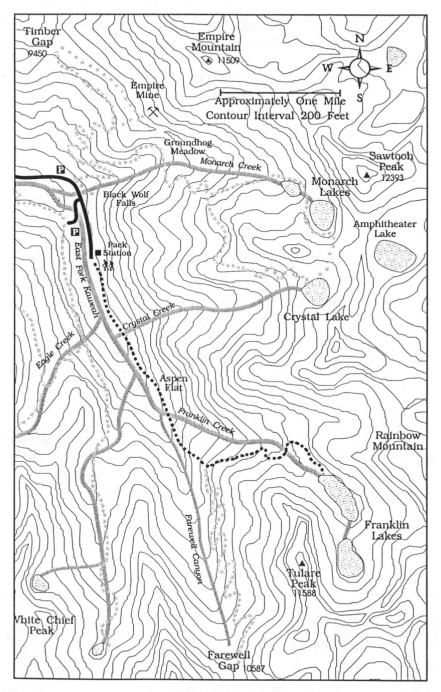

Franklin Lakes Trail

FRANKLIN LAKES TRAIL

DISTANCE: 5 1/2 Miles (one way)
HIKING TIME: 3 Hours (one way)
STARTING ELEVATION: 7850′
HIGHEST ELEVATION: 10,300′
DIFFICULTY: Strenuous to Franklin Lakes
USGS MAP: Mineral King

It's possible to hike from Mineral King to Franklin Lakes and back in a day, but only for a fast hiker, or a slow hiker willing to plod along nonstop all day long. For an overnight backpacking trip, however, this is one of the most popular destinations in Sequoia National Park.

The first 3 1/2 miles of this trail are the same as for the Farewell Gap Trail (see page 161) and therefore won't be described here again.

On the Farewell Gap Trail, at the junction of the Franklin Lakes Trail, elevation 9300 feet, you continue east, climbing gradually into the peculiar red and orange metamorphic rock of Franklin Canyon. If you look carefully on the uphill side of the trail, you can see the shaft and tailings from the Lady Franklin Mine, one of dozens of silver and gold mines in Mineral King.

At about 4 1/2 miles you cross Franklin Creek, elevation 9900 feet. There are flat spots here among the willows that make good places to rest or have lunch. The colorful, 12,000-foot peak to the east is aptly named Rainbow Mountain.

You may be surprised to find a short, man-made rock and mortar dam at the outlet to lower Franklin Lake, elevation 10,300 feet. This dam, and others like it, were built by the Mount Whitney Power Company in 1904, long before this area became part of Sequoia National Park. The idea was to increase the storage capacity of the East Fork's watershed and thereby regulate the water flow into a flume which, even today, runs from Oak Grove to a power generating plant at Hammond, just above Three Rivers. That power plant is now owned by Southern California Edison Company.

The rugged, twisted-looking trees around the edges of the lake are foxtail pines, so named because of the bushy needles at the tips of their limbs.

Upper Franklin Lake is in the bowl to the southeast, about 300 feet higher than the first lake. There's an unmaintained footpath to the upper lake.

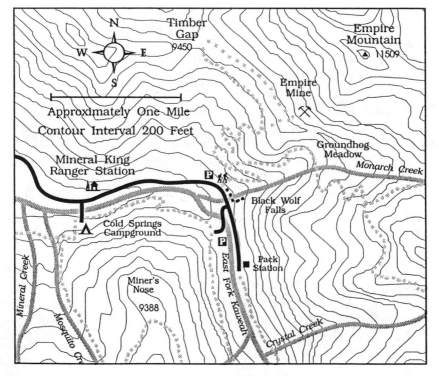

Black Wolf Falls

BLACK WOLF FALLS FOOTPATH

DISTANCE: 1/4 Mile
HIKING TIME: 15 Minutes
STARTING ELEVATION: 7800'
HIGHEST ELEVATION: 7800'
DIFFICULTY: Easy
USGS MAP: Mineral King

You might try this brief hike as a way to cool down at the end of a longer hike. The footpath is not maintained, but the route is safe and easy to follow.

From the Sawtooth parking area, walk south, following the road over the two bridges on Monarch Creek. Looking to the east, you can already see the falls about 500 feet away. Just beyond the bridges you soon come to a gravel wash; a non-maintained footpath begins on the north bank of the wash.

After following the footpath east for 300 feet, you cross the gravel wash, then turn east again. Another 200 feet brings you to Black Wolf Falls.

Here you see the open shaft of what was once a copper mine, just south of the falls. This was called the "Black Wall Falls Mine," named, as you can see, for the dark rock formation. The name "Black Wolf Falls" was probably a misunderstanding, but has now become the accepted name for the falls.

All open mine shafts are dangerous—do not enter this one.

Below the falls are a couple of fair-sized pools.

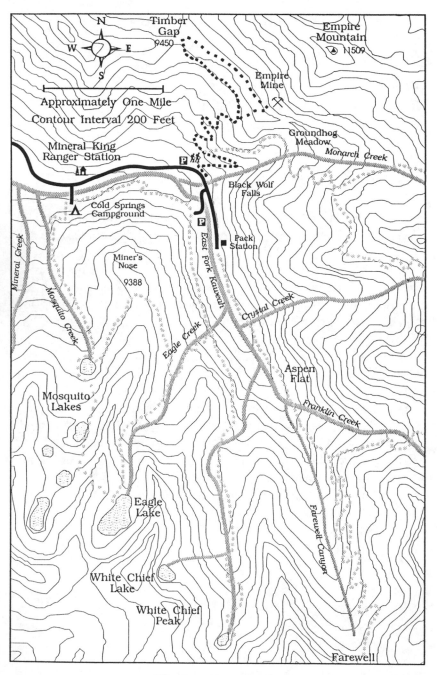

Timber Gap Trail

TIMBER GAP TRAIL

DISTANCE: 2 Miles (one way)
HIKING TIME: 1 1/2 Hours (one way)
STARTING ELEVATION: 7800'
HIGHEST ELEVATION: 9450'
DIFFICULTY: Moderate
USGS MAP: Mineral King

The Timber Gap Trail gives hikers an excellent view of Mineral King Valley and of points to the north. For hikers who wish to venture a ways off the trail, it provides an opportunity to see a historical mining site.

The trail begins at the Sawtooth parking area, .8 miles east of Mineral King ranger station.

The first 1/4 mile of this trail is steeper than most trails, but soon becomes more tolerable. In fact, Timber Gap is the easiest pass leading out of Mineral King. Looking north you can already see Timber Gap, the ribbon of red firs on the saddle above you. As you stop to catch your breath, notice the thick stands of white sage, which are fairly uncommon on the western slope of the Sierra. The entire scene surrounding you, with the open avalanche chutes, quaking aspens, and sage-covered slopes, is much more typical of the eastern side of the Sierra.

Most of the southern Sierra is composed of hard granite which erodes slowly. Mineral King, on the other hand, is composed of softer metamorphic rock that has fractured and eroded so much that all the slopes around the valley consist of loose rock hanging at the angle of repose. That angle is perfect for fostering snow avalanche conditions. On steeper slopes the fresh snow is constantly being sloughed off, while on gentler slopes the fresh snow consolidates into a stable pack; but at Mineral King the snow builds up at a precarious angle until finally its own weight sets off an avalanche. The frequent and sometimes violent avalanches scour the slopes of trees, helping create the sage and aspen look Mineral King is so famous for.

The swiftly flowing creek you see to the southeast is Monarch Creek.

At 1/4 mile you will come to the junction of the Monarch Lakes Trail (see page 173). The Timber Gap Trail continues to your left (north).

The trail now follows short, fairly steep switchbacks through the red firs. At 1 mile you emerge from the trees and follow one long gentle switchback all the way to Timber Gap.

Besides red firs, you also see a few foxtail pines in the gap. Looking to the north, the large drainage you can see below you is Cliff Creek, and the larger drainage beyond that is the Middle Fork of the Kaweah. To the south you can see as far as Farewell Gap.

For those experienced hikers who wish to explore the ruins of the old Empire Mine camp, contour through the trees to the east of the gap, picking your way carefully along the steep and rugged slope, staying at about the same elevation as the gap. After 1/4 mile you emerge from the woods. Stop and look around until you find the remains of an old wagon road—you may see portions of the rock riprap forming the bed of the road. This road was built so that construction timber could be brought from Timber Gap to Empire Mine. The road hasn't been maintained in more than a hundred years, yet it's in surprisingly good condition. As you follow this road to the southeast, if you look straight up the slope of the mountain, about 1000 feet above, you may see the open shaft and mine tailings from the Empire Mine. It was the only mine in Mineral King that ever actually produced silver bullion, though only in very small quantities, and not nearly enough to justify the millions of dollars invested in the mine.

After hiking 3/4 of a mile east of Timber Gap, and just as you enter a strip of red firs, you will begin to see the remains of the old Empire Mine camp: notched logs, red brick from a chimney, part of a cast iron stove, and assorted mining junk. This was the lodging house, destroyed by a snow avalanche on the night of April 16, 1880, with twenty men sleeping inside. Four of the men were badly injured, but miraculously none were killed. That tragedy was the final blow to the Empire Mine. After the summer of 1880, the mine was never worked again.

Most hikers will want to return to Timber Gap and the Sawtooth parking area by the same route as they came. But experienced hikers may want to try the following cross-country route: From the ruins of the Empire Mine camp, carefully pick your way straight down the slope (southwest), staying just inside the strip of red firs. Along the way you may come across pieces of steel cable and other parts of the tramway used to carry ore from the mine to the valley floor. That tramway was designed by Andrew Hallidie, the same engineer who designed San Francisco's system of cable cars. The tram cable was two miles long and supported by timber tripod towers every 200 feet. Ore buckets were attached to the cable, and the weight of the loaded buckets going downhill pulled the empty buckets back up again—sort of a perpetual motion machine if you discounted the labor of the men loading the buckets at the top.

You strike the Timber Gap trail again at an elevation of 9200 feet.

On your descent to the parking area, you can see the remains of an old log cabin. At the end of the long switchback, about 1 mile below Timber Gap and about 200 feet after you re-enter the red firs, look for the cabin about twenty feet below the trail.

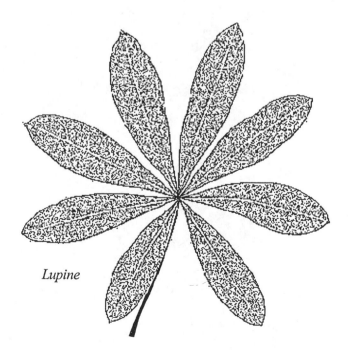

Lupine

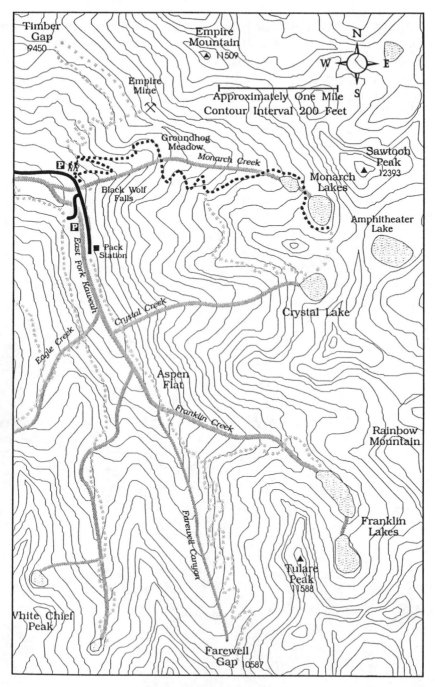

Monarch Lakes Trail

MONARCH LAKES TRAIL

DISTANCE: 4 1/4 Miles (to lower Monarch Lake)
HIKING TIME: 3 1/2 Hours (to lower Monarch Lake)
STARTING ELEVATION: 7800'
HIGHEST ELEVATION: 10,400' (lower Monarch Lake)
DIFFICULTY: Strenuous
USGS MAP: Mineral King

The Monarch Lakes Trail is guaranteed to bring a good night's sleep to even the most hyperactive hiker. Though it's route is fairly steep most of the way, it's also a rewarding hike because of its fine views of the valley and for the diversity of the country it covers. Fishermen sometimes hike up and back in a day.

The trail begins at the Sawtooth parking area, .8 miles east of the Mineral King ranger station. The trail is a bit steep and rough for the first few hundred yards, but soon becomes more reasonable.

As a short and refreshing side trip, or as a complete hike in itself, consider the following: Less than 1/4 mile up the trail you can see a waterfall on Monarch Creek. At a point where the trail switches back to the north, look to your right (southeast) and you will see a narrow footpath which leads to a pool just below the falls. In the summer, this makes a good place to get wet.

At 1/4 mile you come to the junction of the Timber Gap Trail (see page 169). The Monarch Lakes Trail continues to the right (east).

At 1 mile you reach Groundhog Meadow. In the Sierra Nevada groundhogs are more often called marmots. In the eastern states, their cousin is called a woodchuck. People less fond of the marmot sometimes call it a "whistle pig," for its shrill warning cry. This fortunate animal not only has an active social life, but has the good sense to inhabit some of the most beautiful subalpine country in the world. Its thick but coarse fur was never valued by trappers, and its underground habits protect it from most predators as well as from the severe winter cold. Though most people who have tasted the meat of the marmot describe it as greasy, the early miners of Mineral King were said to have practically lived on it.

Just as you cross Monarch Creek, you may see an older trail on the north side of the canyon. That trail is not maintained, is unsafe and should not be used.

As you start up the west-facing slope, you'll pass through a forest of large red firs and junipers. In this area you may come across a family of grouse, brown and gray-speckled birds about the size of a stunted chicken. They're usually seen on the ground and will allow you to come quite close. Most likely you'll hear them before you see them—the males make a strange hooting sound that can be heard miles away. How these rather dimwitted creatures have been able to survive coyotes, bobcats and other predators is a great mystery.

At 3 1/4 miles you will come to the junction of the Crystal Lake Trail (see page 177), elevation 10,000 feet. From this point on the climbing is much more gradual, as you begin a long contour into Monarch Canyon. You pass through an area of red rock, then cross Monarch Creek once again before finally arriving at lower Monarch Lake, elevation 10,400 feet.

Experienced hikers may want to continue on to the upper, larger lake. The footpath begins at the inlet to the lower lake (look for it among the willows) and continues a steep 1/4 mile before coming to upper Monarch Lake, elevation 10,700 feet.

Experienced mountaineers may want to try an alternate route back to the Sawtooth parking area: From upper Monarch Lake, looking almost due south, you see a chute that leads to a saddle on the ridge between Mineral Peak and the Great Western Divide. This chute is steep and narrow but not difficult to climb. Once you have gained the top of the ridge, elevation 11,200 feet, you are looking down on Crystal Lake and Upper Crystal Lake (just a pond, really). A footpath leads from the upper lake, west, over a hump and down to the Crystal Lake Trail. Do not try to hike around the northern end of Crystal Lake—it's too steep. See page 177 for a description of the Crystal Lake Trail, which will return you to the Sawtooth parking area.

Franklin Lake

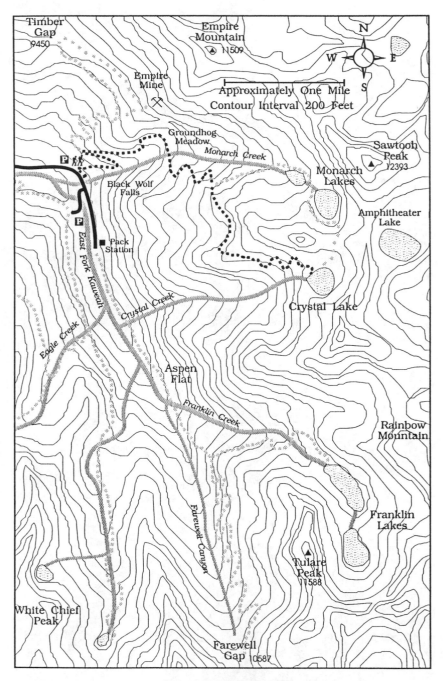

Crystal Lake Trail

CRYSTAL LAKE TRAIL

DISTANCE: 4 1/2 Miles (one way)
HIKING TIME: 3 1/2 Hours (one way)
STARTING ELEVATION: 7800'
HIGHEST ELEVATION: 10,800'
DIFFICULTY: Strenuous
USGS MAP: Mineral King

Many people who have already been to Monarch Lakes will have found that area gets more than its share of hikers. Just a little more effort, however, will take you to Crystal Lake, a very beautiful area that isn't used nearly as much as Monarch Lakes.

The first 3 1/4 miles of this trail are the same as for the Monarch Lakes Trail and therefore won't be described here again (see page 173).

From the junction to Crystal Lake, on the Monarch Lakes Trail, you head southeast, climbing gradually for 1/2 mile into the Chihuahua Bowl, elevation 10,400 feet. On a flat on the south side of the bowl you find the tailings and sealed shaft of the Chihuahua Mine. At one time this historic mine was considered to be one of the best prospects in Mineral King for producing silver and gold. Like all the others, though, it never produced enough to pay for the miners' efforts.

As you leave Chihuahua Bowl you contour around a rugged ridge before entering Crystal Canyon. At about 4 miles you come to the junction of a narrow footpath which leads south to the bottom of the canyon. If you have binoculars, glass the creek and meadow below; it's often crowded with deer, and is also a likely place to spot a mountain lion.

You continue contouring east, climbing gradually to a series of switchbacks on the eastern end of the canyon. From here the trail begins climbing fairly steeply, gaining 500 feet before arriving at the outlet of Crystal Lake, elevation 10,800 feet. The lake itself is barren of trees, so the best places to rest are at the campsites just below the lake, where there are a few gnarled foxtail pines.

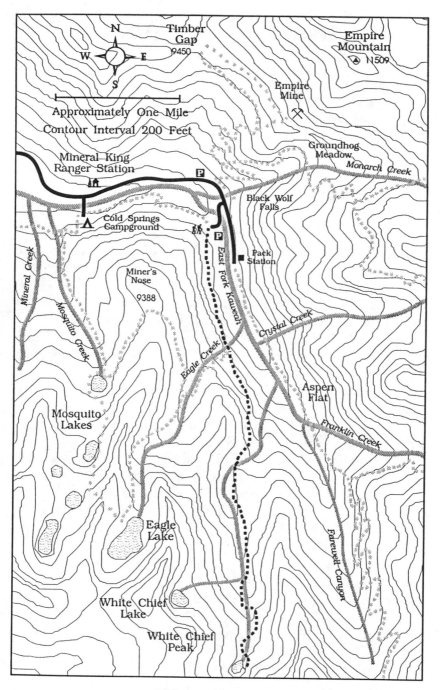

White Chief Trail

WHITE CHIEF TRAIL

DISTANCE: 3 Miles (one way)
HIKING TIME: 2 Hours (one way)
STARTING ELEVATION: 7850'
HIGHEST ELEVATION: 9500'
DIFFICULTY: Moderate
USGS MAP: Mineral King

Although the White Chief Trail is one of the few hikes into the side canyons that does not lead you to a lake, the sight of beautiful White Chief Meadow more than makes up for that. There's also a historical mining site, as well as the remnants of a hundred-year-old cabin.

The trailhead is at the Eagle-Mosquito parking area, 1.2 miles east of the Mineral King ranger station.

The trail begins climbing immediately up the western slope of the valley, passing through stands of red fir as well as some very large junipers. The first water you come to is Spring Creek, which is actually a spring rather than a creek; it emerges from a belt of marble a few hundred feet above the trail.

At 1 mile you come to the junction of the Eagle Lake Trail, elevation 8400 feet (see page 183). The White Chief Trail continues south, traversing up the slope. Across Mineral King Valley, to the east, you can see Crystal Creek, which drains Crystal Lake.

The next mile of trail is the steepest on this hike. Across Mineral King Valley you soon see Franklin Creek, which drains Franklin Lakes.

The trail follows just above White Chief Creek for 1/4 mile or so. There are several places along here to stop, rest and enjoy the view. Notice the stringer meadow on the slope to the south; in the spring and summer a great variety of wildflowers can be seen here.

At 2 miles the trail crosses White Chief Creek. You can now see White Chief Meadow, elevation 9250 feet, a small but fine subalpine meadow with steep talus slopes on the western side. You might smell the minty aroma of pennyroyal growing nearby; it's refreshing to chew and makes an excellent tea.

Stop a few minutes to look for the ruins of the old Crabtree Cabin, which served as a bunkhouse for miners working at the White Chief Mine. The cabin can be found about one hundred feet west of where the trail crosses the creek. You'll see a few notched logs, pieces of a metal chimney and other relics of Mineral King's mining days.

Notice how the nearby meadow is littered with dead trees brought down by snow avalanches. John Crabtree built his cabin well to the north of the meadow because this location is out of danger from avalanches. There are also water and grazing close by, as well as plenty of lodgepole pines—so named because their medium diameter and straight boles are perfect for cabin building.

Another mile brings you to the end of White Chief Meadow, elevation 9500 feet. On the slope to the west, in the white rock just above the chocolate-colored rock, you can see the tailings and several shafts of the old White Chief Mine. The shafts are open and dangerous, and are not recommended for exploring.

The history of the White Chief Mine is as strange as any mine in the West. John Crabtree claimed that he and two other ranchers from the Porterville area, Charles Belden and George Loup, were led to the mine by the spirit of a giant Indian chief. One August night in 1872, they were sitting around their campfire on the Little Kern, south of Farewell Gap. There's no record of what Crabtree and his companions were drinking around the fire that night, but you can bet it wasn't pennyroyal tea. At any rate, this giant Indian chief appeared to them in a vision and asked them to follow him. After an all-night journey the chief brought them to the entrance of a natural cave, where the chief said they would find veins of pure gold.

When Crabtree and the others returned to the San Joaquin Valley, their preposterous story started the first rush of mining fever at Mineral King. Though millions of dollars were eventually invested in the White Chief Mine, it never produced even one bar of silver or gold bullion.

The trail is not maintained beyond the end of the meadow, but experienced hikers may continue following the footpath south to the end of White Chief Canyon, about 4 miles, elevation 10,000 feet. The ruins of several old mining cabins can be found in that area, as well as natural marble caverns.

White Chief Lake is on the bench to the west, 1200 feet above the meadow. There is no trail or footpath, but experienced mountaineers will be able to find a safe cross-country route.

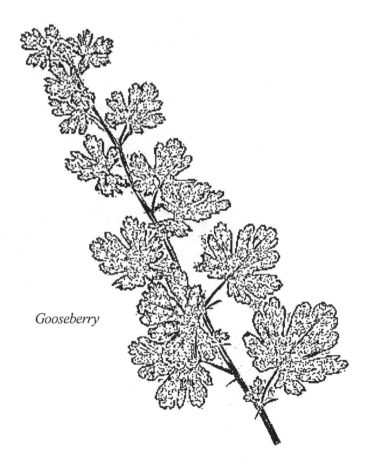

Gooseberry

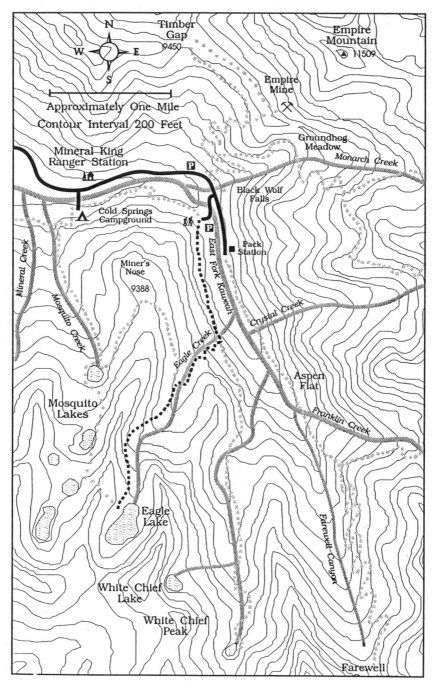

Eagle Lake Trail

EAGLE LAKE TRAIL

DISTANCE: 3 1/2 Miles (one way)
HIKING TIME: 3 Hours (one way)
STARTING ELEVATION: 7850'
HIGHEST ELEVATION: 10,000'
DIFFICULTY: Moderate
USGS MAP: Mineral King

The Eagle Lake Trail is a short but steep route which takes you to one of Mineral King's most popular fishing lakes. The trail begins at the Eagle-Mosquito parking area, 1.2 miles east of the Mineral King ranger station. The trail begins climbing immediately up the west slope of the valley, passing through stands of red fir, as well as some very large junipers. The first water you come to is Spring Creek.

At 1 mile you come to the junction of the White Chief Trail, elevation 8400 feet (see page 179). The Eagle Lake Trail continues to your right (north), climbing short, steep switchbacks.

Looking across Mineral King Valley, you can see a series of peculiar, white rock formations at about the 8500-foot level. That was called Potato Row by the early miners, who imagined that the formations resembled a garden row of potato greens.

At an elevation of 8900 feet, the trail levels off a bit at the entrance to Eagle Canyon, and you soon come to one of the strangest geographical curiosities in Mineral King. Here Eagle Creek disappears into a sink hole. The grayish-white rock around the sink hole is marble; throughout the southern Sierra Nevada caves are found in this formation. Apparently Eagle Creek drains into underground caverns.

Past the sink hole you cross a relatively flat meadow scattered with red firs and lodgepole pines. This makes a good rest area.

At 2 miles you come to the junction of the Mosquito Lakes Trail, elevation 9100 feet (see page 187). The Eagle Lake Trail continues straight ahead (southwest) to an open meadow. Notice the dead trees in the meadow that have been brought down from the rocky slopes above by snow avalanches.

The trail begins climbing steep switchbacks, staying west of Eagle Creek. You soon come to another small flat, but then begin climbing almost immediately again into an area of white granite. In a few places the trail may be difficult to follow through the rocks, so follow the horse-manure markers thoughtfully placed there for your convenience.

And finally you emerge at Eagle Lake, elevation 10,000 feet.

The rock and mortar dam at the outlet of the lake was built there by the Mt. Whitney Power Company in 1905 as a way to regulate the flow of water to their power generating plant at Hammond, above Three Rivers.

Most hikers will want to return by the same route as they came, but experienced mountaineers who feel confident in steep terrain may want to try the following route:

Imagine the dam at Eagle Lake being an arrow pointing west. Beginning at the dam, follow the arrow up the slope through the foxtail pines. After gaining 200 feet in elevation you come to a small grassy bench; looking to your right you see a strip of foxtail pines. Continue west, using the dam below as a guide, until you have gained the top of the ridge, elevation 10,400 feet.

From the ridge you have an excellent view of the Great Western Divide, the Silliman Crest north of Lodgepole, and as far as Kings Canyon. Directly below, you can see the Mosquito Lakes basin. To reach the basin, follow the ridge you are on about 150 feet to the north. You then see a descending ledge that can be followed to the talus slope below. After dropping another 400 feet you come to Mosquito Lake #4. Follow the chain of lakes northward, over a non-maintained footpath, until you strike the Mosquito Lakes Trail (see page 187) at the east end of Mosquito Lake #1. That trail will return you to Mineral King.

(Note: The route described above, from Eagle Lake to Mosquito Lakes, is not a short cut. It will add about two hours to your trip. It is not suitable for inexperienced hikers, but is an opportunity to make an interesting loop out of this hike.)

Mineral King Valley

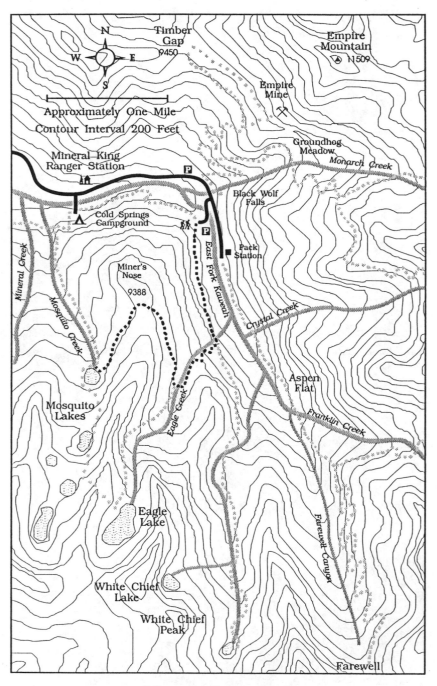

Mosquito Lakes Trail

MOSQUITO LAKES TRAIL

DISTANCE: 3 1/2 Miles (to Mosquito Lake #1)
HIKING TIME: 2 1/2 Hours (one way)
STARTING ELEVATION: 7850'
HIGHEST ELEVATION: 9000'
DIFFICULTY: Moderate
USGS MAP: Mineral King

The Mosquito Lakes Trail is probably the easiest trail out of Mineral King leading to a lake. For that reason it's one of the most popular trails with fishermen. The trailhead is found at the Eagle-Mosquito parking area, 1.2 miles east of the Mineral King ranger station.

The trail begins climbing immediately up the east-facing slope of the valley, passing through stands of red fir as well as some very large junipers. At 1 mile you come to the junction of the White Chief Trail, elevation 8400 feet. The Mosquito Lakes Trail continues to your right (north), climbing short, steep switchbacks.

At an elevation of 8900 feet, the trail levels off a bit at the entrance to Eagle Canyon, and you soon come to the Eagle Creek sink hole, where the creek apparently drains into marble caverns.

Past the sink hole, you cross a relatively flat meadow scattered with red firs and lodgepole pines. This makes a good rest area.

At 2 miles you come to the junction of the Eagle Lake Trail, elevation 9100 feet. The Mosquito Lakes Trail is the right-hand fork (north).

The trail contours around Miner's Ridge, climbing only slightly. At about 3 miles you cross a broad and heavily-wooded saddle between Miner's Ridge and Miner's Nose and begin descending the north slope of Miner's Ridge.

If the Disney Corporation's plans for a major ski resort in Mineral King had become a reality, one of the major ski runs would have been down Miner's Ridge to Mosquito Creek and back to Mineral King Valley.

At 3 1/2 miles you come to the first lake in the basin, Mosquito Lake #1, elevation 9000 feet.

The trail into the Mosquito Lakes basin is not maintained beyond Mosquito Lake #1, but experienced hikers can follow a footpath all the way to Mosquito Lake #5. The route is marked with ducks and with blaze marks on some trees. (Look for the square ax marks about chest high.) Beyond lake #2 the trail becomes more rugged and hard to follow.

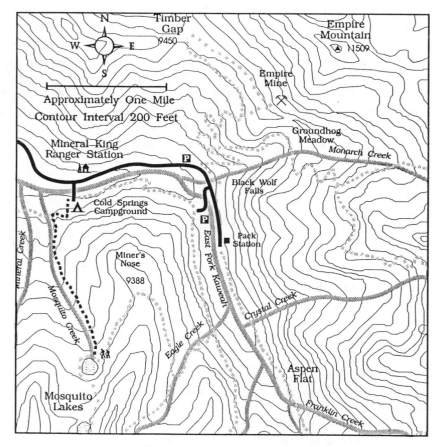

Mosquito Creek Footpath

MOSQUITO CREEK FOOTPATH

DISTANCE: 2 Miles (one way)
HIKING TIME: 1 Hour (one way)
STARTING ELEVATION: 9000'
LOWEST ELEVATION: 7500'
DIFFICULTY: Moderate
USGS MAP: Mineral King

This non-maintained footpath is described here as an alternate route from Mosquito Lakes to Cold Springs campground. But if you like, you can also begin at Cold Springs campground and hike up the beautiful, fern-covered banks of Mosquito Creek. (To begin at Cold Springs campground use the Tar Gap Trail, described on page 191, as far as Mosquito Creek, then hike in reverse the trail described below.)

Starting at the outlet of Mosquito Lake #1, at the north end of the lake, you find a narrow footpath following the route of Mosquito Creek. Follow the creek north, staying on the east side of Mosquito Creek, until you find the remnants of the old trail.

At one time this trail was well traveled, and it is still fairly easy to follow. Several trees have fallen across the trail, but they aren't serious obstacles. Some of the standing trees still have blaze marks.

The footpath drops rapidly, rarely straying more than one hundred feet east of the creek. The lush area surrounding the creek is a good place to spot wildlife, so watch carefully. There are also several small pools for fishing or swimming.

Pay careful attention at the point where the footpath passes through thick willows—it's easy to lose the route there.

After 1 1/4 miles, you strike the Tar Gap Trail, elevation 7800 feet. Turn right (east) and follow the trail 1/2 mile to Cold Springs campground.

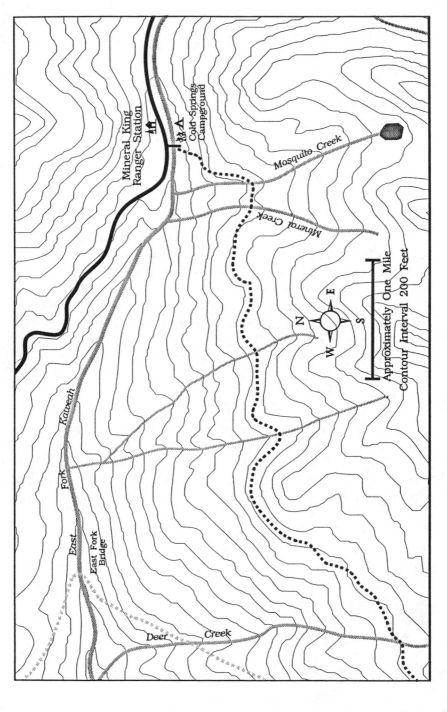

Tar Gap Trail

TAR GAP TRAIL

DISTANCE: 3 1/2 Miles (to Deer Creek)
HIKING TIME: 2 1/2 Hours (one way)
STARTING ELEVATION: 7500'
HIGHEST ELEVATION: 8200'
DIFFICULTY: Moderate
USGS MAP: Mineral King

The Tar Gap Trail is used mostly by stock users riding into Hockett Meadow, but it also makes a fine day hike for the first few miles. The views aren't as spectacular as you might find in Mineral King Valley, but the solitude found here is excellent.

Mule packers often use this trail for day hikes too, though few will admit it. Pack stock turned loose at Hockett Meadow will sometimes return all the way to Mineral King. Packers who let the sound of their mare's bell get too far away in the night have to get out of bed at dawn and follow their stock on foot twelve miles back to Mineral King.

The Tar Gap Trail begins at the west end of Cold Springs campground. Unless you're staying at the campground, leave your car at the Tar Gap Trail parking area, .2 miles east of the Mineral King ranger station and .5 miles east of this trailhead.

After leaving the campground, the trail begins climbing through a thick forest of both white and red firs. The trail is a bit steep, but the grade soon becomes more gradual. At 1/4 mile you cross an unnamed creek.

At 1/2 mile you come to Mosquito Creek. There are small fish in the creek and occasional pools for swimming. This makes a good destination for a short hike. As you cross Mosquito Creek you may see thimbleberry, a bright green plant with red berries, almost like a raspberry; thimbleberries are one of the most delicious berries in the Sierra.

There's a non-maintained footpath that follows the east side of Mosquito Creek. It's not difficult to follow; see page 189 for a description of its route.

At 3/4 miles you come to Mineral Creek, elevation 8100 feet. The vegetation along this creek is very lush, which makes a pleasant contrast to the rockier Mineral King Valley. After Mineral Creek the trail becomes much less steep as it contours around the side of the mountain. For several miles now this trail is just a pleasant stroll, with hardly any elevation gain.

1 3/4 miles brings you to a long stringer meadow, thick with willows. A bit farther, as you look above the trail, you'll see an open avalanche chute and some rocky crags above that; this is the end of the arc of peaks surrounding Mineral King Valley.

At 2 3/4 miles, after passing a second stringer meadow, you begin to round the point of the mountain and head in a southwesterly direction. If you look below the trail, to the northwest, you may see the tops of some giant sequoias. They're part of the East Fork Grove, also described on the Atwell to Hockett Trail.

And 3 1/2 miles brings you to Deer Creek, elevation 8200 feet. There are good places to rest here along a steep stringer meadow. You will find water in the creek, even in the driest years.

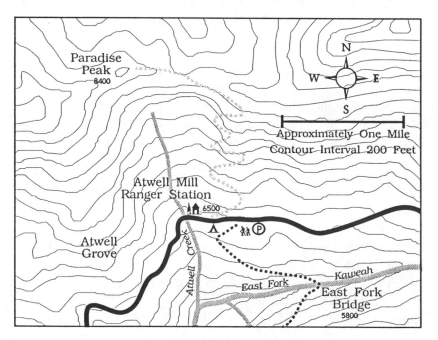

Atwell to Hockett Trail

ATWELL to HOCKETT TRAIL

DISTANCE: 2 Miles (to Deer Creek)
HIKING TIME: 1 1/2 Hours (one way)
STARTING ELEVATION: 6500 '
LOWEST ELEVATION: 5800 '
DIFFICULTY: Moderate
USGS MAP: Mineral King

This trail leads to a grove of sequoias not seen by most visitors to the park and along the way crosses a beautiful river canyon. To make an excellent day hike for children, go only as far as the bridge over the East Fork.

The trail begins at the west end of Atwell Mill campground. Unless you're staying at the campground, you must leave your car at the parking area at the east end of the campground, 1/4 mile away.

As you leave the campground, hiking west, you soon come to a small meadow near the old Atwell Mill. Skirt the left side of the meadow (south), and you soon see a trailhead sign which reads, "Hockett Meadow."

While you're at Atwell Mill, take a few minutes to look at the old machinery left from the logging days, as well as the huge sequoia stumps. Logging began here in the 1870s to supply the miners at Mineral King with lumber. In 1886, after most of the mines had gone bust, A.J. Atwell, a retired judge from Visalia, started the mill which you can still see pieces of now. If it hadn't been for the conservation movement in the last part of the Nineteenth Century, most of the giant sequoias in this park might have been reduced to the stumps you see here. The wood of giant sequoias is too brittle for most construction purposes; most often the largest trees on earth were bucked into short lengths, then split into fence posts, roof shingles and grape stakes.

As you start down the trail, heading southeast, you pass through a great variety of conifers: ponderosa pine, sugar pine, white fir, cedar and sequoia. You also see an ankle-high shrub with sticky leaves and a very strong "woodsy" aroma. It has at least three common names:

mountain misery, bear clover, and the Miwok Indian name, kit-kit-dizze.

This trail is frequently traveled by black bears. If you keep your eyes open you may spot one, particularly in the early morning or evening. Look for their tracks in the soft dirt along the trail. The hind track looks something like a barefoot human's track; if you look carefully you can even see the creases in the sole. The front track is oval, with five toe prints.

At about 1/2 mile you begin to hear the roar of the East Fork of the Kaweah to your south. You come to a small creek with a short waterfall and a sequoia on the ledge above it. The shrub growing in the creek bed is thimbleberry, which produces a sweet fruit almost like a raspberry. Just past this creek crossing, a careful eye might spot a trace of an old, no-longer-maintained trail which leads to Cabin Cove.

By 3/4 of a mile you begin to see the white granite channel of the East Fork. And at 1 mile you come to the bridge over the East Fork of the Kaweah, elevation 5800 feet. With the waterfall above, and the surrounding sequoias, this is one of the most scenic destinations in the Mineral King area.

The banks of the river are too steep and slippery for swimming or fishing. Do not attempt to walk down to the water.

Crossing the East Fork bridge and continuing up the south side of the canyon, you pass through the East Fork Grove. The trail soon becomes moderately steep, as it passes through the heart of the grove, before reaching Deer Creek, 2 miles, elevation 6500 feet.

Hockett Meadow, where the Park Service has a backcountry ranger station, is about another 10 miles.

East Fork Bridge in Winter

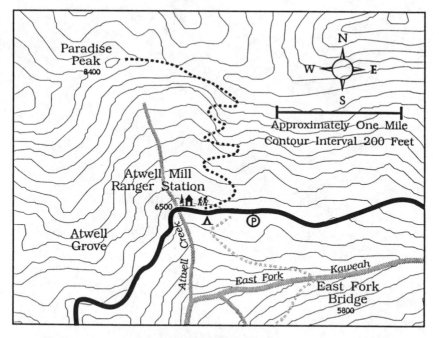

Paradise Ridge Trail

PARADISE RIDGE TRAIL

DISTANCE: 2 Miles (one way)
HIKING TIME: 3 Hours (one way)
STARTING ELEVATION: 6500'
HIGHEST ELEVATION: 8400'
DIFFICULTY: Strenuous
USGS MAP: Mineral King

This trail is traveled mostly by stock users riding from Atwell Mill to Cliff Creek. It's rarely used by backpackers, who prefer to reach Cliff Creek by way of Timber Gap. The trail is steep (nearly a 2000-foot gain in 2 miles), fairly dry, and most day hikers probably won't want to continue all the way to the top of the ridge. Still, an interesting short hike can be made to a seldom-seen area of Atwell Grove. Since it's hot here in the summer, hikers should consider a morning hike, or perhaps an early evening hike to watch the sunset. Remember to carry water.

This trail begins at Atwell Mill. There's a sign marking the trail on the north side of the road, .2 miles east of the Atwell ranger station, or .1 mile west of the entrance to Atwell campground. Unless you're staying at the campground, leave your car at the parking area .2 miles east of the campground.

The trail begins by climbing through a mixed conifer forest of sugar pines, white firs, cedars, ponderosa pines and young sequoias. Look to the ridge a mile to the west, across Atwell Creek, and you may be able to see the silhouettes of giant sequoias against the skyline. Mature sequoias have a rounded top, while most other conifers are pointed and more symmetrical.

You pass through some thick patches of manzanita, with red bark and bright green leaves. The Indians made a drink from the berries of manzanita by crushing the berries in a mortar, then placing the berries in a basket and pouring cool water through them. Early white settlers said this manzanita cider was the most refreshing drink they'd ever tasted. The berries themselves are also edible; they have a large seed and just a thin skin of flesh, but that doesn't stop black bears from eating them by the mouthful. If you see any bear scat along this trail, you'll notice that manzanita berries make up a large part of their diet.

At 1/2 mile you begin to see some large sequoias. Above the trail is an interesting grove of perhaps a dozen medium-size sequoias, all within fifty feet of each other. Farther on there are even larger sequoias.

You cross a small creek, or spring, elevation 7200 feet, with bright green ferns growing along the bottom. This makes a good turnaround point for a short hike, but you may continue as far as you like. The trail follows long, steep switchbacks to the top of Paradise Ridge.

As a historical note to this trail, in the 1930s the government seriously considered building a road from Lake Isabella, up the Kern and Little Kern, through Hockett Meadow to Atwell Mill, and then over Paradise Ridge to Redwood Meadow and on to Giant Forest. At one time the Park Service even set aside $15 million to begin the road, but the superintendent of Sequoia National Park, Colonel John White, flatly refused to accept the money, citing the irreparable harm it would do to Sequoia's vast backcountry. Because of White's stubbornness and foresight, Sequoia remains one of the few national parks in the West without a major thoroughfare slashing through the heart of it.

APPENDIX 1: BEST SWIMMING HOLES

Waterfalls, deep clear pools and sparkling creeks are among this park's most popular hiking destinations. It's always refreshing to stop on a hike long enough to get wet, and after a hike a brief dip can be re-invigorating. Except for those pools in the lower foothills, though, there are very few swimming holes in the park warm enough to actually swim in. The high country lakes look tempting, but both the high altitude and the frigid water temperatures will take your breath away. It's not advisable to swim in the high lakes. More suitable are the smaller pools along the many creeks and rivers described in this guidebook.

All the swimming areas described in this guidebook have some degree of danger. Rivers in the Sierra Nevada are cold and swift, and the river banks tend to be steep, rocky and slick. Every year park visitors lose their lives in the park's rivers, so use extreme caution, particularly in the spring and early summer when water levels are high. Diving from the banks is particularly hazardous. There have been many head and neck injuries in the park as a result of this foolish and unnecessary activity. Diving from the banks should be strictly avoided.

The following swimming holes are listed by area and then by the trail which will take you there:

Giant Forest

Sugar Pine Trail: at Crescent Creek, small but sunny pools

Lodgepole

• Tokopah Falls Trail: along the Marble Fork, very cold water, medium-size pools

Dorst Creek

• Lost Grove Trail: at Dorst Creek, small to medium-size pools

• Cabin Creek Trail: at Dorst Creek, small to medium-size pools

Mineral King

• Cold Springs Trail: on the East Fork, small to medium-size pools, cold water

• Farewell Gap Trail: on the East Fork at Aspen Flat, small pools, cold water

• Franklin Lakes Trail: on Franklin Creek, small pool, cold water

• Monarch Lakes Trail: on Monarch Creek, small pool at 1/4 mile, cold water

• Black Wolf Falls: on Monarch Creek, small pools, cold water

Foothills

• Indian Head Swimming Hole: on the Middle Fork, very large pool

• Potwisha Pictographs Loop: on the Middle Fork, several medium-size pools

• Hospital Rock Swimming Hole: on the Middle Fork, several large pools

• Paradise Creek Trail: at the Middle Fork bridge, large pool; along Paradise Creek, several small pools

• Ladybug Trail: on the South Fork, several small to medium-size pools

• North Fork Trail: on the North Fork, medium-size pools; on Yucca Creek, some medium-size pools

APPENDIX 2: BEST FISHING SPOTS

The fishing areas described here are a mixture of rugged areas for the skilled fisherman and easily-reached areas intended for the less experienced fisherman or for fishermen with children. By reading the description for each suggested trail, you can pick a fishing spot that suits your needs. Each area described can produce fish for the competent fisherman, but the more remote and rugged areas often produce more and larger fish.

Fishing regulations for Sequoia National Park change from time to time and are quite complicated. If you plan to fish, stop by one of the visitor centers or ranger stations for a copy of the fishing regulations and read it thoroughly.

The following fishing spots are listed by area, and then by the trail which will take you there.

Giant Forest

- Marble Fork Bridge Trail: at the Marble Fork Bridge, good fishing below the bridge but very rugged, not suitable for children.

Lodgepole

- Tokopah Falls Trail: on the Marble Fork, small fish but a good place for kids

- Twin Lakes Trail: on Clover Creek

- Lakes Trail: Pear Lake, Aster Lake, both heavily used

- Clover Creek Footpath: on the Marble Fork, very rugged

- Lodgepole to Wolverton Trail: on Wolverton Creek, small fish

Dorst Creek

- Lost Grove Trail: at Dorst Creek, small fish but usually good for kids

Mineral King

- Cold Springs Trail: on the East Fork, good fly-fishing area

- Monarch Lakes Trail: Monarch Lakes

- Crystal Lakes Trail: Crystal Lake

- Eagle Lake Trail: Eagle Lake

- Mosquito Lakes Trail: Mosquito Lakes, easiest hike to lakes from Mineral King

- White Chief Trail: rugged cross-country route to White Chief Lake

Foothills

- Lookout Point Trail: on the lower East Fork

- Potwisha Pictographs Loop: on the Middle Fork at the suspension bridge

- Hospital Rock Swimming Hole: on the Middle Fork

- Paradise Creek Trail: on the Middle Fork at the foot bridge

- Marble Fork Trail: on the Marble Fork, at the end of the trail, very rugged, not suitable for children

- Ladybug Trail: along the South Fork

- North Fork Trail: along the North Fork

APPENDIX 3: BEST TRAILS FOR GIANT SEQUOIAS

Giant Forest

- Crescent Meadow Trail: Tharp's Log, Chimney Tree

- Congress Trail: Sherman Tree, Mckinley Tree, General Lee Tree, House Group

- Huckleberry Trail: Washington Tree, Bears' Bathtub, Dead Giant

- Trail of the Sequoias: Chief Sequoyah Tree, Senate Group

- Soldiers Trail: Roosevelt Tree, Triple Tree, Parker Group, Broken Arrow

- Wolverton Cutoff: on the edge of Giant Forest Grove

Dorst Creek
- Lost Grove Trail: Lost Grove

- Muir Grove Trail: Muir Grove

Mineral King
- Atwell to Hockett Trail: Deer Creek Grove

- Paradise Ridge Trail: Atwell Grove

Foothills
- Ladybug Trail: lowest-elevation sequoias in the world

- Garfield-Hockett Trail: one of the largest groves in the park

APPENDIX 4: BEST HIKES FOR CHILDREN

The trails listed below are all less than 2 miles in length, are all classified as easy, and are interesting and instructional for children under ten years old.

Giant Forest
- Round Meadow Loop: a self-guided nature trail

- Hazelwood Trail: a self-guided nature trail

- Congress Trail: a self-guided nature trail

Lodgepole

● Tokopah Falls Trail

● Long Meadow Loop

Dorst Creek

● Lost Grove Trail: as far as Dorst Creek

Mineral King

● Cold Springs Trail: a self-guided nature trail

● Farewell Gap Trail: as far as Aspen Flat

● Tar Gap Trail: as far as Mosquito Creek

● Atwell to Hockett Trail: as far as the East Fork bridge

Foothills

● Potwisha Pictographs Loop

● Hospital Rock: pictographs

● Paradise Creek Trail: for the first mile

● Ladybug Trail: for the first 1 3/4 miles

APPENDIX 5: BEST HISTORICAL SITES

● Crescent Meadow Trail: Tharp's Log

● Huckleberry Trail: Squatters Cabin

● Trail of the Sequoias: Tharp's Log, Cattle Cabin

● Soldiers Trail: Soldiers Camp

● Colony Mill Road: Colony Mill

- Cold Springs Trail: site of Beulah mining town

- Timber Gap Trail: site of Empire Mine camp

- Crystal Lake Trail: site of Chihuahua Mine

- White Chief Trail: Crabtree Cabin and White Chief Mine

- North Fork Trail: Yucca Flat

APPENDIX 6: BEST WATERFALLS

- Tokopah Falls Trail

- Black Wolf Falls Footpath

- Atwell to Hockett Trail: at the East Fork bridge

- Middle Fork Trail: at Panther Creek

- Marble Fork Trail: at Marble Falls

APPENDIX 7: BEST VIEWS

- Marble Fork Bridge Trail: Sunset Rock

- Moro Rock Climb: Moro Rock

- Soldiers Trail: Hanging Rock, Moro Rock

- Sugar Pine Trail: Bobcat Point

- High Sierra Trail: Eagle View

- Wolverton Cutoff: one mile north of High Sierra Trail

- Alta Trail: Panther Gap, Alta Peak

- Lakes Trail: the Watchtower

- Twin Lakes Trail: JO Pass

- Muir Grove Trail: granite dome at 1 mile

- Little Baldy Trail: best view of any day hike in the park

- Farewell Gap Trail: at the gap

- Timber Gap Trail: at the gap

- Monarch Lakes Trail: first two miles

APPENDIX 8: CAMPGROUNDS IN SEQUOIA

Only Lodgepole Campground accepts reservations, all others are on a first-come basis. For Lodgepole information call (209) 565-3774.

- Potwisha Campground: On the Generals Highway, four miles from the Ash Mountain entrance station. 44 sites, water, restrooms, dump station, no reservations

- Buckeye Flat Campground: one mile east of Hospital Rock, on a narrow side road, 28 sites, no trailers or RVs, no reservations, water, restrooms

- South Fork Campground: on South Fork Road 13 miles east of Highway 198 and Three Rivers, 13 sites, pit toilets, not recommended for trailers or RVs, no reservations

- Atwell Mill Campground: on the Mineral King Road 19 miles from Highway 198, 21 sites, pit toilets, no reservations, not recommended for trailers

- Cold Springs Campground: on the Mineral King Road 23 miles from Highway 198, 37 sites, pit toilets, no reservations, not recommended for trailers

- Lodgepole Campground: at Lodgepole, 260 sites, water, dump station, restrooms, reservations accepted

- Dorst Campground: at Dorst Creek, 218 sites, water, dump station, restrooms

- Stony Creek Campground: in Sequoia National Forest (outside the park), on the Generals Highway 2 miles north of Lost Grove, restrooms, water, for reservations call (800) 280-2267

APPENDIX 9: MILEAGE IN SEQUOIA

On The Generals Highway:

Ash Mountain Entrance Station	0.0	Miles
Ash Mountain Visitor Center	0.7	
Potwisha	3.8	
Hospital Rock	6.1	
Crystal Cave Road	14.6	
Giant Forest Village	16.7	
Sherman Tree Parking Area	19.0	
Wolverton Road Junction	19.5	
Lodgepole	21.0	
Clover Creek	21.8	
Little Baldy Saddle	27.4	
Dorst Campground	28.9	
Lost Grove	31.5	

On The Mineral King Road:

Junction with Highway 198	0.0	Miles
Lookout Point	10.3	
Atwell Mill	19.0	
Mineral King Ranger Station	23.4	

APPENDIX 10: PHONE NUMBERS

Emergencies	911
Sequoia National Park, information	(209) 565-3134
Sequoia National Park, main number	(209) 565-3341
Weather & Road Conditions in the park	(209) 565-3351
California Road Conditions (Caltrans)	1-800-427-7623
Park Lodging	(209) 565-3314
Foothills Visitor Center	(209) 565-3134
Lodgepole Visitor Center	(209) 565-3782
Lodgepole Camping Reservations	(209) 565-3774
Lodgepole Chevron Station	(209) 565-3381
Mineral King Ranger Station	(209) 565-3768
Silver City Resort	(209) 561-3223

APPENDIX 11: FISHING REGULATIONS FOR SEQUOIA & KINGS CANYON NATIONAL PARKS

Fishing Licenses

A California State Fishing License is required for everyone aged 16 or older. Licenses are generally available at concession markets located in the National Parks.

Fishing Season

Trout: Last Saturday in April through November 15. Exceptions: All lakes and the South Fork Kings River from the Park boundary to Bubbs Creek open all year.

Other Species: Open season all year.

Limit of Catch and Gear

Below 9,000-foot elevation and not in an Exempted Area

Native Species: Zero Limit (catch and release fishing only). This includes rainbow trout and non-game species like Sacramento sucker, sculpin, and roach.

Introduced Species:

Trout: 5 trout per day/10 in possession. This includes brown trout, eastern brook trout, and golden trout.

Green sunfish and black bullhead: No limit. These species are only found in the North Fork Kaweah.

Only barbless hooks and artificial flies and lures are permitted.

Above 9,000-foot elevation or in an Exempted Area

Trout: 5 trout per day/10 in possession.

Other species: no limit.

Barbed or barbless hooks. Bait, artificial flies or lures are permitted.

Exceptions:

Summit Lake and other waters of the North Fork Tule River
   Limit: 2 trout. *Only artificial flies permitted.*

South Fork Kings River
   Park boundary to Copper Creek: 2 trout. *Bait and barbed hooks permitted.*
   Copper Creek to Bubbs Creek: zero rainbow trout, 2 of other trout species. *Only artificial lures with barbless hooks permitted.*
   Kern River from Park boundary to Tyndall Creek
   Limit: 2 rainbow trout 10 inches or less total length. *Only artificial lures with barbless hooks permitted.*
   Special brook trout bonus bag and possession limit: up to 10 brook trout per day less than 8 inches total length may be taken and possessed in addition to the other daily bag and possession limits.

Closures

Soda Springs Creek in southern Sequoia National Park is closed to fishing to protect a sensitive population of Little Kern golden trout.

Exempted Areas

These areas are exempt from catch-and-release requirements:
   (a) Kern River drainage (see special regulations above);
   (b) South Fork Kaweah River and tributaries upstream from 7600 foot elevation;
   (c) South Fork Kaweah River from Park boundary to Clough Cave footbridge;
   (d) Waters upstream from confluence of Whitman and Horse Creeks in the East Fork Kaweah drainage;
   (e) East Fork Kaweah River and tributaries upstream from Mosquito Creek;
   (f) Kaweah River from Park boundary to water diversions on Middle and Marble Forks;
   (g) Middle Fork Kaweah River from first highway parking area west of Hospital Rock to first footbridge above Buckeye Campground;
   (h) Marble Fork Kaweah River upstream from Silliman Creek;
   (i) Dorst Creek from Cabin Creek to Generals Highway;
   (j) Creeks at Grant Grove area south to Dry Creek drainage;
   (k) Roaring River drainage;
   (l) South Fork Kings River from the Park boundary to the confluence with Copper creek. This stretch subject to 2-trout limit.

Other Rules

Fish may be taken only by angling with one (or two in lakes) closely attended rod and line or one hand-line with not more than three hooks nor more than three artificial lures. (Each lure may have three hooks attached.)

Drugs, poisons, explosives, electricity, and chumming are prohibited.

Digging or gathering any natural bait (including worms, mollusks, and insects) is prohibited within these Parks.

Live or dead minnows or other bait fish, amphibians, and non-preserved fish eggs or roe are prohibited.

Fishing from road bridges is prohibited.

Comments

Within these Parks, golden trout are native only to Soda Springs Creek and the Kern River. The form of golden trout that is native to the Kern is known as Kern rainbow. Other forms of golden and rainbow trout were introduced into the Kern drainage.

Where hybrids may occur between rainbow and golden trout, regulations will be enforced on the basis of which species the take most resembles.

Index

About the Author

Steve Sorensen worked in the resources management division at Sequoia and Kings Canyon National Parks for fourteen years, followed by several years as a journalist. He now lives in Three Rivers, California, just outside of Sequoia, with his wife and two sons.

To Order:

Day Hiking Sequoia

or the companion volume

Day Hiking Kings Canyon

Please send $14.00 per copy, check or money order, to:

Fuyu Press
PO Box 720
Three Rivers, CA 93271

Price includes tax and shipping